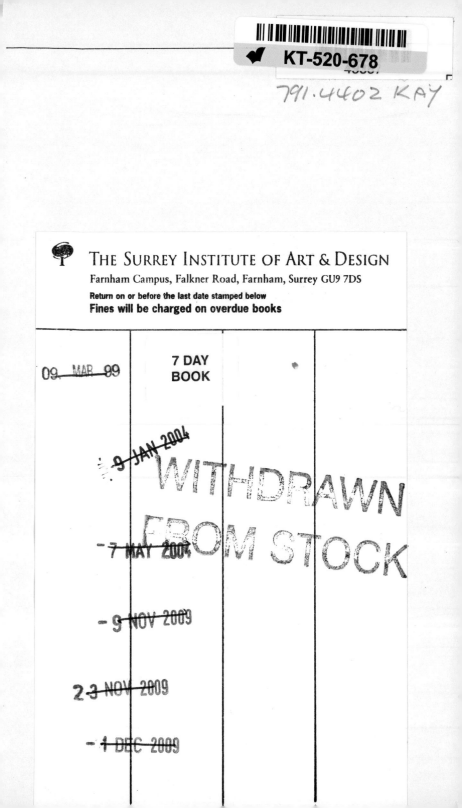

Making Radio

A GUIDE TO BASIC BROADCASTING PRODUCTION AND TECHNIQUES

Michael Kaye and Andrew Popperwell of the BBC World Service

BROADSIDE BOOKS LIMITED

ACKNOWLEDGMENTS

We would like to thank colleagues in the BBC World Service, particularly George Albone, for proof-reading the text and helping us with the production of the cassette. The information contained in 'Making Radio' forms part of the Basic Radio Production Course we run at Morley College in London. We owe a great debt to the students of that college for allowing us to use and abuse their material. Of course, our heartfelt gratitude goes to Catherine Bradley, our publisher, without whom 'Making Radio' would not have seen the light of day.

First published 1992 by
Broadside Books Limited
2 Gurney Road
London E15 1SH

ISBN 1874092 001

Printed and bound in Great Britain by Bookcraft (Bath) Ltd.

Design by John Meek

CONTENTS

1 WHY RADIO?

RADIO is the media genie, small enough to fit into a bottle, big enough to cover continents. At one end of the scale there are radio stations in locations as specific as hospitals; at the other, world services that live up to their name, spanning the globe. Every size of audience, from a few dozen to millions.

Radio has developed into the most intimate of the media, the principal one-to-one means of communication. At the same time, in remote agricultural communities the radio receiver may still be the focus of family life (as it was during the Second World War in Europe), gathering people to listen to news that affects all their lives.

Although television is now the most popular form of home entertainment, radio has not disappeared, as some people in the nineteen fifties predicted. There are times in life when television is simply out of the question. Watching a picture while driving along an autobahn might prove a short-lived undertaking, but the traveller still requires up-to-date information.

And in spite of CDs and cassettes, listening to someone else's choice of music still pleases a vast audience. The element of surprise is a potent attraction and more and more stations are moving to a looser schedule of music and speech that keeps the listeners guessing.

Radio also gives the listeners access — not just to more music than anyone could hope to hear in a lifetime, but to the people who shape our lives, the politicians, the business executives, the artists, the entertainers.

Communication has become a genuine two-way traffic in modern radio. Thanks to the phone-in, your views can find an outlet. For all kinds of reasons, radio wants you to talk back. You may write letters to a newspaper editor or make an angry phone call to a television station but, so far, radio is the best option for you to speak your mind publicly and easily.

Radio has other advantages over its rivals. Television is the only medium that can rival radio's speed of delivery. However, television is many times more expensive than radio. A major conflict can beggar a television news operation in weeks.

A celebrated radio presenter hit the headlines when it was reported that he was about to earn £200,000 a year for fronting a show for a big commercial radio station in London. Nice for him.

Nicer still for the station. They had signed a performer who could not only attract listeners for several hours each day but could also fill those hours without too much additional expense. If you divide all those accumulated hours by the salary, the result is bargain broadcasting. For the equivalent sum you could purchase one hour of a television wild-life documentary. At the most basic level, radio gives us the information we require to pursue our daily lives: weather reports, travel conditions, food prices, the time of day. It can also be much more.

Another way of describing radio is by the ratio of speech to music. The least expensive form of radio is the computerised juke-box. There are stations of non-stop popular music that require an engineer to visit them only once a day - to switch them on. Advertisements may come as a welcome relief. From there it's a small step each time to add time checks, station identification, brief news, weather and traffic bulletins.

Why, you may ask, would anyone wish to run a station that restricts itself to music and the minimum of speech? In one word – money. Even though radio is very cheap, the shrewd commercial broadcaster wishes to minimise costs and maximise profits. Speech radio costs much more than recorded music.

But in the end the audience can insist on more variety in its radio. There is greater competition for the listener's ear today and the broadcaster who does not respond to demand will go under.

The wonderful and difficult thing about the radio audience is the growing sophistication of its taste. No station can be all things to all listeners, try as it might. When radio began it tried to supply a service to please everyone. The break-up of the old public-service monopolies and the rapid growth of small commercial and community stations means a growing specialisation: stations for the jazz addict, the serious-music lover, the under-fives, the over seventy-fives.

This means more and more ways of making radio and more and more opportunities to do so. The old-established speech radio forms, the documentary, the feature, drama, the discussion, the magazine are still flourishing, sometimes under different names.

The values and styles of radio developed since the 1920s still hold good today. The idea that radio should inform, educate and entertain still lurks in the back of broadcasters' minds. Nowadays, broadcasters still debate the question of whether the public should listen to what they want or what is good for them.The range of skills required by the broadcaster varies. The smaller the station, the wider the range of activities each broadcaster is expected to tackle.

In long-established public-service networks, a broadcaster may never appear in front of a microphone. On a small community radio station, people do everything in front of and behind the microphone, including publicity, cleaning the studio and making the tea.

In an industry of such diversity and range the opportunities are limited only by your ability to exploit them. Although the best way to learn radio is to do it, it won't harm your chances if you already have the basic information you require.

Now read on.

2 THE CHAIN LETTER

2.1 FROM MOUTH TO EAR

Radio at its most basic is one person talking to another. What gets the sound from the speaker to the listener?

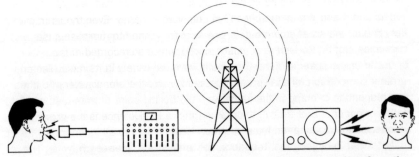

● You start with the vocal chords, which vibrate when you speak to form the sound waves in the air, which then spread out in all directions.

● Then there's the microphone, which simply converts these sound waves into electricity, which runs down the cable to the...

● Mixing desk, where other sounds (from other microphones, or records, or tapes) are added. From which the sound runs along a wire to the...

● Transmitter, which in turn converts the electrical signals into radio waves which spill out into the ether from an aerial (antenna) system. The transmitter may be long, medium or short wave (AM, or Amplitude Modulation), or VHF (Very High Frequency), also known as FM (Frequency Modulation).

● The waves spread out, usually in all directions, for a distance that varies according to the power and location of the transmitter, the frequency of the transmission, and the shape of the land. Mountains, for example, will block out FM stations very successfully!

● Next, the radio receiver's aerial (antenna) picks up the transmitted radio waves, and the electronics inside the radio convert them into an audio signal which the loudspeaker or headphones convert back to airborne sound waves...

● ...which are then heard and analysed by the listener's ears and brain.

2.2 WAVELENGTHS AND FREQUENCIES

Sound consists of vibrations in the air. We count the number of vibrations – waves – which happen in one second, and call this the frequency of the sound.

The higher the frequency, the higher the pitch. Think of running a stick along railings. Then run faster!

These frequencies are measured in cycles per second, more usually called Hertz, abbreviated Hz. A thousand make a kiloHertz (kHz), and a million a megaHertz (MHz).

The lowest note you can hear is about 30Hz, and the highest is about 18kHz. As you get older, this upper limit falls. It falls faster if you work unprotected in a noisy environment, or go to too many loud concerts.Radio waves are a part of the electromagnetic spectrum, which also includes light, microwaves, infra-red, ultra-violet, X-rays, etc.

Radio waves are similar to sound waves, except that they don't need air to travel in. And they have a much higher frequency.

Frequency and Wavelength: If a given number of sound waves arrive at your ear (or radio waves at your radio) in one second – then that number is the frequency. But if they have a constant speed (which they do, either the speed of sound or the speed of light) then each wave will have a certain wavelength.

So you can also call a particular frequency by a particular wavelength. It's just a question of units. In the same way, the boiling point of water can be called either 100°C or 212°F. Your radio may be marked in either system. Frequency is becoming the more common term.

Note that the higher the frequency, the smaller the wavelength.

2.3 BROADCASTING FREQUENCIES:

Radio is broadcast in four different wave-bands:

Long Wave, that is, low frequency; for example, BBC Radio Four on 1515 metres or 198kHz.

Medium Wave, that is, medium frequency; for example, BBC Radio Three on 247 metres or 1215kHz.

Short Wave, that is, high frequency; for example, BBC World Service on 6.195 MHz or 49 metres.

Very High Frequency, VHF, also called FM (Frequency Modulation); for example, Jazz FM on 102.2 MHz.

Television is broadcast on yet higher frequencies – UHF, or Ultra High Frequency, and satellites are further up still, in the 12 gigaHertz range (giga = thousand million).

2.4 DISTANCE:

Long wave will travel several hundred miles, medium perhaps a hundred or two, while short wave and VHF are limited to about 50 miles. Community stations use low-power transmitters with a range of a few miles.

However, short waves have the unexpected property that they will bounce off a layer high in the sky, the ionosphere, and come down thousands of miles away. This allows international broadcasting, with only the hindrance of poor quality caused by the interference and fading that the volatile nature of the ionosphere generates.

2.5 FM AND AM:

These stand for Frequency Modulation and Amplitude Modulation respectively. They are just two different ways of putting a sound signal onto a radio wave. FM is used only on VHF, which is why some radios are labelled this way. FM is capable of much higher quality than AM, carrying a greater range of audio frequencies and suffering much less from interference.

Stereo: basically, VHF/FM is the only transmission system in current UK use that has enough room in the radio signal for the extra information content needed for stereo. So stereo is always on VHF, and never on long, medium or short wave.

And of course radio can arrive at the listener's home via cable systems or by satellite.

3 ARTFUL NOISE: ACOUSTICS AND STUDIOS

3.1 ACOUSTICS

If you went blindfold into a room you'd never entered before, and someone spoke to you, you'd know two things immediately:

- How far away the person was, and
- What sort of room it was – a bathroom would sound quite different from a bedroom, for example.

This is because of the way the ear sorts out direct and indirect sounds. When a person speaks (or any other sound is created), the sound waves in the air spread out in all directions, just like the ripples on a pond when you throw in a stone. In an ordinary room, these sounds will bounce off the walls, floors and ceiling, and will thus spread rapidly to fill the whole room.

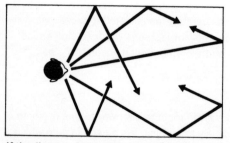

If the listener is close to the speaker, most of the sound heard will come directly from the speaker's mouth, and very little relatively will be indirect, that is, bounced off the walls or ceiling.

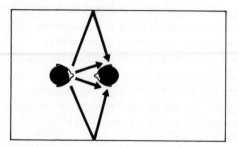

If the listener is far from the speaker, the opposite applies: most of the sound heard is indirect.

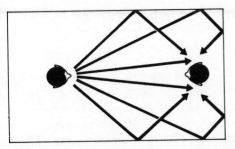

It is the ratio of direct to indirect sound which tells the listener how far away the speaker is.

The quality of the reflected, indirect sound will tell the listener something about the room: obviously, in a very large room, like a cathedral or a concert hall, the indirect sound will have travelled a large distance before it is reflected. This takes a finite time, and in the extreme case is perceived as a distinct echo.

Also, stone walls or wood-panelled surfaces reflect sound more efficiently than, for example, curtains, carpets and other soft furnishings. So a tiled bathroom sounds quite different – much more 'live' – than a bedroom of the same size.

In radio drama, these effects are deliberately manipulated to create the various sets for the necessary scenes. Movable screens with one side sound-reflective – a hard wooden surface – and the other sound-absorptive – soft wadding – form the acoustic scenery.

3.2   REVERBERATION TIME

This is the time taken for a sound in a given room to die away to one millionth of its original loudness, that is, effectively to nothing. It's a useful figure which can give an idea of the acoustic properties and 'feel' of the room.

- A typical living-room might have a reverberation time of 0.5 seconds.
- A typical concert hall might have a reverberation time of 1.5 to 2.5 seconds.
- A typical cathedral might have a reverberation time of 5 to 8 seconds.
- A typical radio studio might have a reverberation time of 0.3 seconds.

The idea behind such a short reverberation time for a radio studio, that is, such a 'dead' acoustic, is that since the listener's room at home will have an acoustic of its own which will affect the sound coming out of the radio loudspeaker, then having as little 'original room' on the sound makes sense. Otherwise, the sound arriving at the listener's ear will have a mixture of two distinct acoustics – unpleasant and tiring to listen to, as well as less intelligible in more extreme cases.

Artificial reverberation: for drama and music, it's sometimes necessary to create a longer reverberation time than the studio provides naturally. There are many commercial devices available: the basic rule is that the more you pay, the better the simulation.

3.3 STUDIOS

So what makes a studio a studio? Three main properties:

● Sound isolation. The studio walls, floor and ceiling are built so that as little sound as possible leaks in from the outside, and in particular between the Control Room and the Studio proper (see below). So footsteps in the corridor outside will be inaudible, as will a telephone in the adjacent office or an aeroplane flying overhead.

● Good acoustics. As described in 3.2 above, it's important that the studio is as 'dry' as is reasonably practicable. If the acoustic treatment is overdone, this can make for a rather claustrophobic working environment.

● Technology. While there's no reason why you can't just lash up the necessary equipment in any acoustically suitable room, it's usual to make a more permanent installation by building-in microphone sockets, clocks, red lights, sound-mixing desks and so on. And it's much neater if the hundreds of cables needed are hidden in trunking built into the walls, or under the floor.

A basic studio looks like this:

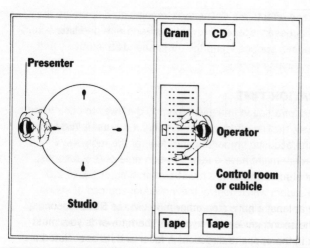

The key features are:

● The Studio itself, where the presenter(s) and guests sit, and where the microphones are placed. There will be accurate clocks, red lights, head-phones, a loudspeaker, cue lights (usually green) and soft-topped tables.

● The Control Room, where the Producer sits, together with the Engineer (or, in the BBC, the Studio Manager). There will be clocks, red lights, head phones, loudspeakers, and a lot more technical equipment: a mixing desk, tape recorders, record and CD players, cartridge machines etc.

In smaller radio stations it's normal for the presenter also to have a mixing desk. And there may be no engineer, and sometimes no separate producer.

In stations with their own news service, there's often a separate small news-reading studio, which can be faded up (made audible) on the main sound desk at the appropriate time.

All areas are usually connected by double- (or, better, triple-) glazed windows, which allow easy visual communication. And there's always 'talkback', a push-button intercom system which is connected to the headphones and loud-speakers in the various areas.

Also, all areas will probably be connected to a central apparatus or 'racks' room, where the connections to other studio centres, to transmitters, and to telephone links can be made.

3.4 MIXING DESKS

The sound-mixing desk is the heart of any radio studio. It is used to mix together all the different components of the programme. This means both sequentially, when one item after another is adjusted so that the whole programme flows smoothly, and also simultaneously, when several sounds are superimposed on one another – a disc-jockey talking over a record, for example.

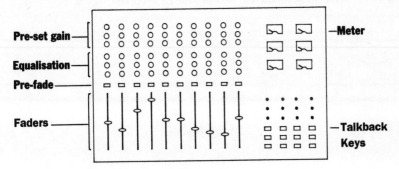

The main features of a sound desk:

● Faders are the sliders which control the individual sources of sound. There are usually at least eight, often many more. In the BBC, faders generally make the sound louder when you pull them towards you; most other desks work in the opposite direction! A fader and its associated pre-fade, equalisation and similar controls are often referred to as a channel.

● Jackfields or patchbays are lots of sockets which you interconnect with short lengths of flex with a plug on each end. These are called double-enders, or patchcords. The idea is that you can plug any sound-source to any fader you choose. For example, conventionally, many people put micro-phones to the left-hand channels and records and tapes to the right.

● Equalisation controls, or EQ, are tone controls similar to those on a hi-fi. There's usually one set for each fader, except on the simplest desks. EQ allows sounds to be matched in quality, so that they sound the same. It also permits improvement of poor-quality sound – from a scratchy old record, for example, or a hissy tape. Beware – it's very easy to reach for the EQ knobs to try to fix a microphone sound problem. It's much better to go and adjust the microphone itself!

● Meters allow the loudness of a programme to be monitored and controlled accurately. See Section 4 on Loudness, Levels and Meters.

● Talkback keys and microphones let the producer or engineer communicate with the presenter. Usually, the presenter cannot hear talkback if the microphone is on ('faded up') unless headphones are worn. Otherwise, the talkback would be heard by listeners!

● Pre-fade controls allow you to listen to something before you fade it up on air. For example, you could check the first few words of the next tape while the previous one is still playing.

● Red lights often come on automatically when you open a microphone. There may also be a separate switch to turn them on.

● Cue lights, often green, are operated either by opening a microphone fader or by operating a switch (sometimes a foot-switch). These tell the presenter when to start talking, and sometimes when to stop (e.g. one green flick for 30 seconds left, and two for 15 seconds).

4 THE EXPLODING PIN: LOUDNESS, LEVELS AND METERS

4.1 LOUDNESS

Drop a pin. Not very loud, is it? Stand next to a road-drill in action. Painful, isn't it? The difference in loudness between these two sounds – one that can only just be detected by the human ear, and one that can damage it – is staggering.

The road drill is about 10,000,000,000,000 times louder than the pin dropping.

It's extremely difficult to design electronic systems which can imitate real life's enormous range. The limiting factors are distortion at the loud end (turn a cheap radio up loud and see how awful it sounds) and unwanted noise at the quiet end (tape in particular has an inevitable built-in hiss).

So, in broadcasting, as well as in hi-fi, the trick is to make the quiet bits louder so that they are no longer lost in the noise, and the loud bits quieter, so that they don't distort.

To do this, we need some system for metering the sound level as it passes through the mixing desk. No practical system can cope with the ten-million-million range described above. To overcome this problem, we have to use another sort of unit, the deciBel.

4.2 THE DECIBEL

10,000,000,000,000. First, count the zeros. There are thirteen. Then, design a meter calibrated from 0 to 13. Call the units Bels, after Alexander Graham Bell. So far, so good. But it turns out that this is not a particularly convenient unit. So, divide the Bel into tenths, and call them deciBels, abbreviated dB (deci = one tenth). Thus the scale now reads 0 to 130.

Since, as mentioned in Section 4.1, no electronic system can cover this whole real-life range, choose the important section in the middle, between the distortion and the hiss.

One final point about deciBels: they're relative units, not absolute units. So when you say that a sound is 65dB, it's generally taken to mean that it's 65dB louder than the threshold of hearing – the pin dropping. And because of the huge range they cover, adding three Db is the same as doubling the loudness of the sound.

So a jet taking off is, say, twice as loud as a road-drill – and a test-meter calibrated against the threshold of hearing will register 133dB against 130dB. But both are pretty painful!

4.3 PRACTICAL DECIBEL RANGES

- 'Real life'   130dB
- Hi-fi   50 – 60dB
- Professional audio   60 – 70dB
- Cheap cassette machine   30 – 40dB
- CD Player   90dB+

So the CD player puts equipment significantly better than a professional analogue tape recorder into the home! And the latest digital professional equipment is all in the CD class at well over 90dB.

4.4 TRANSMISSION DECIBEL RANGES

- AM Broadcasting (long, medium & short-wave)   20 – 30dB
- FM Broadcasting (VHF)   50 – 60dB

4.5 METERS

Most hi-fi systems contain a meter for setting recording levels; this is almost invariably a VU, or Volume-Unit meter. It's often made with a red and white scale, although many newer models have a line of lights (LEDs, or light-emitting diodes) rather than a needle.

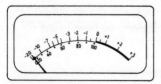

The VU is inaccurate, tiring to watch, and is inconsistent in that it may be constructed and adjusted in various different ways. A much better device is the PPM, or Peak Programme Meter.

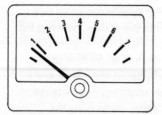

This is made so that the needle rises quickly yet falls back slowly. This means that it shows the peak loudness more accurately – it flaps about much less – and it is less tiring to watch. The PPM is constructed and adjusted to a scientific standard, so it is absolutely consistent, too. There are 4dB between each pair of markings on the PPM scale.

The maximum level is PPM6, that is, the sound should not cause the meter needle to exceed 6 on the scale. The minimum depends on the type of programme material, and its destination: speech for a short-wave broadcast should always peak to PPM6, whereas a quiet passage of classical music for an FM stereo broadcast may well be below PPM2 for half a minute or more. And the key point is that, as the name suggests, the PPM monitors the peaks of the programme loudness.

Practical PPM use: keep the peaks between 4 and 6. The odd overshoot will do no harm, but consistent or excessive overpeaking should be avoided.

When setting-up a sound mixing desk for a programme, adjust the preset gain controls so that the faders give you the right loudness for each sound-source when they are about three-quarters open. This way there's a bit in hand if the source gets quieter, and there's plenty of fader for a neat and elegant fade-out on, say, a piece of music.

[PPM4 has special significance: it's used for engineering tests using a special sound called 'tone', which is a fixed note of 1,000Hz (1kHz). It always reads PPM4, and can be used, for example, to check that a line between two studios is properly adjusted.]

4.6   BALANCE

When taking levels before transmission or recording, that is, checking the loud-ness of all the components of the programme, you may notice that two voices look the same on the PPM, but one of them sounds distinctly louder than the other. This is because of their different sound-qualities. And it shows once again how the ear is different from an electronic device.

The solution to the problem is to let the ear judge, and to adjust the faders so that the two voices sound the same. And that's because the other object of the exercise, apart from avoiding the noise and distortion problems, is to set your levels so that the listener at home can sit back and enjoy your programme without having to keep adjusting the volume on his or her radio.

Taking this idea a stage further, a little more thought is required for music-and-speech programmes: because music is a continuous sound, it feels psychologically louder than a voice. So the usual custom, which 'sounds' right, is to peak the presenter to PPM6, and the music to about PPM4. Some music – loud orchestral, or heavy metal – can also peak to 6, while other music – solo guitar, or harpsichord – is better at PPM2 to 3. But 'Speech to 6, music to 4' is a useful guideline.

5 CARDIOID SURGERY: MICROPHONES

5.1 WHAT THE MICROPHONE DOES

The microphone turns sound waves in the air into electricity, which can be amplified, recorded, broadcast and so on. The main difference between the microphone and the ear is that the ear is controlled and interpreted by the brain, while the microphone is not.

The microphone is a very stupid device. This means that if, for example, you talk to someone across a chattering crowd at a party, then you'll still be able to understand what they are saying. Listen to the output of a microphone in the same place, and all you'll hear is a hopeless muddle of sound.

The brain has helped the ear to sort out the wanted sound from the unwanted.

Returning to the diagrams in Section 3.1, if we place a microphone in the listener's position instead of ears, then whereas the listener had no difficulty in either position, the microphone output in diagram 3 will sound much more distant, containing more 'acoustic', or indirect sound, and will be harder to listen to.

There are many different makes and types of microphone, from large, expensive stereo models used for symphony orchestras to tiny tie-clip versions popular on television.

The most important property, apart from reasonable sound quality, is the pick-up pattern.

5.2 PICK-UP PATTERNS

All microphones sound different, and some are better for one task than
another. The most important property of a microphone is its 'Directivity
Pattern', sometimes called its 'Polar Diagram'. All this means is the direction
in which it picks up sound.

There are:

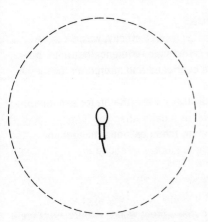

Omni-directional microphones – sometimes called uni-directional. These pick
up sounds equally in all directions, so you can place one between two or more
speakers and, providing all voices are the same loudness, they will all be
heard equally.

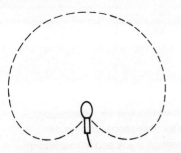

Uni-directional microphones – sometimes called cardioid. These pick up in just
one direction, and you need one for each speaker in a multi-presenter
programme. They're called cardioid because it's Latin for heart-shaped, which
is what an engineering drawing of their pick-up pattern looks like.

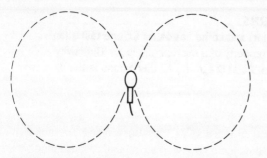

Bi-directional microphones – sometimes called figure-of-eight. These are often flat-shaped, rather than cylindrical, and they pick up sound on both faces, but not on the edges. You can have two presenters, one each side. They're called figure-of-eight because an engineering drawing of their pick-up pattern looks like an 8.

Switchable microphones. These can be switched between the various directivity patterns – they are expensive!

5.3 MICROPHONE POWERING

Some microphones, those that work on the 'capacitor', 'electrostatic' or 'electret' principle, need electric power to make them work. Sometimes there's a small battery built in – remember to turn off after use. More expensive and sophisticated versions use power from the sound mixing desk. There's no separate cable – the electricity flows along the same wires as the audio signal, and is cleverly prevented from interfering with the sound. This method is called 'phantom powering'.

A phantom-powered microphone won't work into a portable tape recorder unless it's an expensive one which will provide the necessary voltage.

Don't forget – in radio, it doesn't matter what a microphone looks like, it's what it sounds like that counts!

5.4 MICROPHONE TECHNIQUE

To avoid a poor acoustic, you need to work relatively close to the microphone. But if you get too close, then you may well suffer from 'pops' on plosive consonants like p, b and t. When you see pop-singers practically swallowing their microphones, remember that they're using an altogether different technique for very different reasons, and their mics are specially designed for this.

Also, some microphones can sound very 'bassy' if you get too close. This is particularly true of bi-directional ones. The best working distance is between 15 and 45 centimetres, or 6 to 18 inches.

Finally, microphones are also sensitive to damp and wind noise. So keep them out of the wind and rain.

6 MIX AND MATCH: MORE ABOUT USING THE SOUND DESK

THIS SECTION assumes that you have to operate the mixer yourself. Traditionally, this hasn't been the way that producers have worked in large broadcasting organisations like the BBC. In the commercial world, however, getting your hands on the equipment is taken for granted – there's rarely a dedicated studio manager or sound engineer. And indeed the BBC is also moving in this direction.

Using a sound desk for straightforward purposes is really quite easy. The most important thing is to set it up the way you want, keeping everything as simple as possible within the needs of your particular programme.

6.1 SETTING UP THE MIXER

The first thing to do is to set all the knobs and switches to their 'zero' or normal position. This will save much confusion later.

Next, you need to decide which sound-source will appear on which channel. Unless the installation is fixed and unalterable, it's best to put all the microphones on, say, the left, and other sources – usually tapes and discs – on the right. Since most programmes follow the sequence Narrator – Tape – Narrator – Disc or something similar, setting the desk up as described means that you'll be working alternately with your left and right hands, and that your sitting position will be comfortable and relaxed.

As already mentioned, adjust the preset gain controls so that the faders are about three-quarters open when the sound is at the right level.

6.2 USING THE FADERS

One of the principal rules of sound desks is that all faders should be shut unless there's a reason for them to be open. Observe this rule and there will be far fewer unexpected intrusions into your programmes.

All faders for speech-microphones should be open to full volume or shut. This is because speech is always heard at full level (except perhaps in drama). Note that this doesn't necessarily mean that the fader is open as far as it will go – rather, as far as is needed to provide full loudness. Music and sound effects, however, can have faders at any point. It just has to sound right.

Make sure that if speech and music or effects are happening at the same time that the speech is clear and intelligible; there's nothing more off-putting to your listener than having to struggle to understand what's being said through the mush. And just because it sounds all right in your studio, where you're listening in optimum conditions, doesn't mean that it will sound the same after radio transmission has introduced its normal hisses and interference.

6.3   THE SEAMLESS ROBE

The trick with operating the faders is to avoid any aural gaps between items, and maintain a smooth control of level. The art is to disguise the technology, so that everything flows naturally.

That's why it's vital to take level before you get going.

6.4   TAKING LEVEL

Taking level is listening to the first few seconds (and possibly the last few as well) of each component of your programme. This enables you to do two things:

● To write down on the script how far open the fader has to be if the sound is to maintain the optimum loudness, and

● To check that the sound is good, and if necessary to do something to improve it. For example, you might need to use the equalisation controls (see below) to reduce the hissiness of a tape.

Running through the items in a typical magazine programme will take just a couple of minutes, and will pay dividends. You may also notice if a cue doesn't fit with the first few words on tape, or, worse, that it's the wrong tape altogether.

Disc-jockeys routinely check the beginning of the next disc while the previous one is playing. The button on the desk labelled PFL (Pre-Fade Listen) enables them – or you – to check level without putting the music on the air.

6.5   EQUALISATION

Steer well clear of the equalisation controls unless you really know what you're doing. They are mainly there to improve poor-quality sound – and it's far better to avoid these problems altogether by making sure you start with a good sound. It's the old principle of 'Garbage In, Garbage Out'.

That said, you'll find the equalisation controls most useful for:

● Removing tape hiss by turning down the treble

● Removing traffic rumble by turning down the bass

● Making a speaker's voice sound a little more intimate by increasing the 'presence' – the band of frequencies in the middle range.

But you never get something for nothing – attempting to remove an unwanted sound will always take away something from the sound you do want.

6.6   PAPERING OVER THE CRACKS

An item on tape is ending. You don't wait until the red trailer is winding through the tape machine before you open the presenter's microphone fader – that way, there will be a moment of absolute silence in between the two sounds.

What you do is rather to open the microphone a few seconds early, warning the presenter just before you do so. Something like 'Coming soon' will make sure that s/he stops coughing, sharpening a pencil or whatever it might be, so that the moment the tape ends the presenter can pick up the thread smartly.

And it's vice versa at the end of the live link. Start the tape or disc as soon as the presenter has concluded the cue, but wait until the new sound is established before closing the microphone fader.

All programmes have a natural pace, and items will follow their cues either immediately or after a shorter or longer pause. It's up to the producer and studio manager to make this happen. But the same principle of opening microphones before inserts end, and closing them after a new insert has started, always applies.

Note that it's up to the studio manager to flash the cue light at the presenter, to indicate 'Talk!', but the fader must always be opened first, rather than the other way round, otherwise the presenter will sound as though s/he is fading in from very far away.

7 GETTING IT TAPED: TAPE AND TAPE RECORDERS

7.1 TAPE

Tape is just thin plastic coated with tiny particles of iron oxide, chrome oxide or plain metal itself. In other words, in its simplest form, it's just rusty plastic! It comes in several formats:

- Quarter-inch is the standard reel-to-reel or open-reel format. It has the advantage that it's easy to edit with a razor blade, and the disadvantage that it's expensive.

- Cartridges contain quarter-inch tape in an endless loop ranging from a few seconds' to a few minutes' duration. They are widely used for stings and jingles. The tape cannot be edited.

- Cassettes contain tape an eighth of an inch wide. It is cheap, but cannot be cut-edited. With some cassette machines, dub-editing, that is, accurate copying of selected parts of a recording, is possible.

- Multitrack tape is used for complex music recording, with up to 24 separate sound-tracks across the tape. It ranges from half to two inches in width, and is not usually cut-edited.

- Video tape, either on cheap cassettes or expensive open-reel format, works in essentially the same way as audio tape. However, the mechanics of the recording system are more complicated, in order to store the huge amount of information that a picture contains compared with a sound-only recording. There are one or two hybrid formats, where this extra capacity is exploited to record sound only using very high quality digital techniques.

- The DAT system (Digital Audio Tape) uses a cassette smaller than a conventional one, but which uses adapted computer and video technology to provide an extremely high quality digital sound. Once again, it cannot be cut-edited, although quite sophisticated dub-editing is possible.

- Computer discs can be used to store sound in digital form at high quality. This is generally extremely expensive, but is capable of very sophisticated computer-controlled editing.

7.2 THE BASIC ANALOGUE SYSTEM

The heart of any tape recorder is the head. This is a small electromagnet, curved round to form a circle, with the tiniest of gaps between the ends:

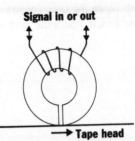

Signal in or out

→ Tape head

An ordinary domestic tape-recorder, either open-reel or cassette, will have two heads. The first erases the tape (wipes it of any previous recording). The second either records or plays back the sound, depending on which button you press.

A professional tape-recorder, and indeed some up-market cassette machines, will have three heads: one to erase, as before, one to record, and a separate one to play back. This splitting of the record and playback functions is for two reasons:

● Better quality is possible, because each head can be better engineered, with less compromise.

● Off-tape monitoring is possible, that is, listening to the replay head (the recording) while the sound is actually being recorded at the record head. This means that you don't have to listen to the whole programme after the recording just to make sure it's there – you spot any technical problems the instant they happen. Doing this does, however, introduce a small delay into the sound – the time the tape takes to travel from the record head to the replay head.

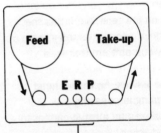

Feed   Take-up

E R P

Erase, Record, Playback heads

Action point: it's vital that tape heads, and indeed all other parts of the tape transport mechanism, are kept scrupulously clean, so that good sound quality is maintained. Cotton buds and cleaning fluid applied gently at regular intervals will do the trick.

7.3 HOW THE TAPE HOLDS THE SOUND

The tape coating can be imagined as millions of tiny bar-magnets. On an unused tape, these particles are randomly arranged. When the tape passes over the record head, the magnets are realigned into ordered patterns, and the sound is stored.

Recorded tape: order

Blank tape: disorder

7.4 HOW THE HEADS WORK

As mentioned above, the head is just an electromagnet. When the sound signal (in electrical form, of course) arrives at the coil of wire, it turns the C-shaped metal part into a temporary and varying magnet. The lines of force (remember the iron filings at school?) run between the two poles. Now, these two poles are very close – perhaps a hundredth of a millimetre apart. So the lines of force are extremely short, and hence very concentrated.

The tiny magnetic particles on the tape are thus subjected to a very strong force, and they line themselves up to form an ordered pattern along the tape, instead of the random muddle which was there before.

This is the principle of the record head.

The erase head works in the same way, except that it uses an extremely high frequency signal, typically 80 kiloHertz, which is way beyond the range of human hearing. It's also too high to be recorded on the tape, but it has the effect of giving all the little magnetic particles a 'kick', and so jumbles them up and randomises their orientation so that any previous pattern, that is, a recording, is destroyed.

The playback or replay head works in the same way as the record head except in reverse – the pattern of little magnetic particles passing over the head-gap sets up a magnetic field which in turn causes an electric current to flow in the coil of wire, which is then amplified and so on.

7.4 BIAS

To make a substantial improvement to the sound quality of a tape-recorder, a very small amount of the erase signal is added to the sound as it arrives at the record head. In simple terms, this extra ingredient helps to get the tiny magnetic particles into motion – it overcomes their natural inertia. But it's vital that you have exactly the right amount of this so-called bias. That's why it's important to set your cassette machine accurately for the type of tape you're using – ferric or chrome etc. And if you're getting poor quality recordings, in spite of having cleaned the mechanism thoroughly, it may be that your machine's bias needs adjusting – this is a job for a specialist.

7.5 NOISE REDUCTION SYSTEMS

The laws of physics mean that all tape suffers from a background hiss (see 7.6 below). As this is a particular problem with cassettes, most such recorders feature clever systems that reduce this effect. The best-known is probably Dolby-B, but there are several other types. If your tape-recorder has such a system, then use it – but make sure that you note on the cassette which system you've used, and check that the machine it's going to be played back on also has the same system – otherwise you won't achieve the quality you need.

7.6 POINTS TO NOTE WHEN RECORDING

There are two major problems with the tape-recording process:
- If you record too loudly, there just isn't the capacity in the tiny magnetic particles to hold that much sound. Result – distortion.
- On the other hand, all tape hisses. This means that if you record too quietly, then you'll end up with a sound which is swamped by the underlying hiss which has become intrusive.

The trick is to hold the middle ground – equally far from both the hiss and the overload distortion. See also the section on levels.

7.7 TAPE SPEEDS

The faster the tape, the higher the quality (and the greater the cost!). Quarter-inch tape can be used at 3.75, 7.5 or 15 inches per second (ips) (9.5, 19 or 38 centimetres per second).
- 3.75 ips is too slow for reliability and good quality, and it makes editing very fiddly.
- 7.5 ips is a good compromise, and is the standard speed for almost all professional radio work.
- 15 ips is used for radio drama and music because of its high quality.

It can be a little cumbersome to edit, as quite long pieces of tape represent quite short sounds!

7.8 TAPE DURATIONS

- A 5-inch spool at 7.5 ips will last 15 minutes (600 feet).
- A 7-inch spool at 7.5 ips will last 30 minutes (1200 feet).
- A 10.5-inch spool at 7.5 ips will last 1 hour (2400 feet).

These durations apply only to standard-play tape. Long-play and similar types are thinner, so that you get more on a spool, but they are more liable to stretch, and infinitely harder to edit. Not recommended!

Cassettes always work at 1 7/8 ips – much slower than open-reel. They are, however, capable of very good quality. This is mainly because of some clever electronics, particularly the noise-reduction systems mentioned above. They cannot be cut-edited.

As with open-reel tapes, cassettes come in various durations. The best are the C60s – 30 minutes on each side – and the worst are the C120s – 60 minutes on each side. As above, stick to the shorter lengths.

7.9   ACTION POINTS:

- Take care when handling tape not to stretch or crease it.
- Take care not to place tapes close to a magnet – it will at least partially erase them. Since all loudspeakers contain magnets, never store tapes next to them. And remember, when travelling, that electric trains have motors with powerful magnets – so avoid the carriages with motors beneath them, and keep the tape off the floor. If necessary, stand up to hold your bag.
- Keep the mechanism clean, and keep the machine covered when not in use, so that dust can't enter.
- If quality begins to deteriorate, get the bias and also the alignment of the heads checked out – this last is critical, and is a specialist's job to remedy.
- Don't forget to label tapes clearly with what's on them, and the date, and for cassettes, which sort of noise-reduction you've used.
- Whatever the spool-size of the recorded material, your empty take-up spool should match. Uneven sizes upset the tension on some machines, causing speed-variations.

8 YOU CAN TAKE IT WITH YOU: PORTABLE TAPE RECORDERS

8.1 CASSETTE OR OPEN-REEL?

Advantages of cassette:
- Light weight.
- Batteries last well.
- Can record up to 90 minutes on a cassette.
- Relatively cheap equipment.
- Cassettes are cheap and freely available.

Disadvantages of cassette:
- Can't be edited – must be dubbed (copied) to open-reel first.
- Very small loudspeaker, sometimes headphones only.
- Not important-looking!

Advantages of open-reel:
- Can be edited immediately – no need to dub.
- Looks 'professional'.

Disadvantages of open-reel:
- Heavy weight.
- Batteries don't last long.
- Tapes only last 15 minutes.
- Tape expensive, not freely available.
- Machines expensive.

8.2 WHERE TO RECORD?

When you use a portable tape recorder on location, the room you use and the technique you use are far more important than the actual machine, provided of course that it's in reasonable condition with fresh batteries. The aim is to make the room as much like a real studio as possible. This means:
- Good acoustics – little echo or reverberation, and
- Good sound insulation from unwanted noises.

So:
- Choose a room with plenty of soft furnishings, carpets, curtains etc.
- Avoid tiles, vinyl floors, panelled walls etc.
- Close all windows and curtains.
- Avoid the centre of the room – that's where the acoustics are likely to be worst, since reflected sounds are concentrated there.
- Take the telephone off the hook.
- Stop people in adjacent rooms from typing or playing the piano.

- Listen carefully during the interview for unwanted noises – an aeroplane passing overhead will sound much more prominent, and will make editing difficult.
- Don't interview across a hard table – it will reflect sound unpleasantly.

8.3 CHECKING THE EQUIPMENT

Operating the gear must be second nature. You must practise beforehand, so that you don't make embarrassing mistakes in front of your interviewee. The other things to get right before you set off are:

- Check the batteries – and take a spare set.
- Take as much tape as you could possibly need – and then an extra reel.
- Check that the microphone is working, and that all the leads and plugs are the correct ones, and that everything works properly.

8.4 GETTING SET UP

Having chosen a suitable room, find a good place to set up your interview:

- Place two chairs fairly close together at right angles.
- Put the tape recorder where you can see it, so that you can keep an eye on levels, and also make sure the reels are turning. If possible, try to keep the machine out of your interviewee's sightline, to avoid any distraction.
- Plug in the microphone and do a quick test recording. Play it back.
- If using an open-reel machine, make sure it's set to 7.5 ips (19 cm/s).
- If using a cassette machine, make sure it's set for the sort of tape you're using (ferric, chrome or metal) and that whatever sort of noise-reduction (Dolby etc) you need is switched in.
- Find a comfortable, relaxed position in which to hold the microphone so that it is roughly halfway between you and the interviewee.
- Take level on both voices – the old 'What did you have for breakfast?' routine.
- Adjust the recording volume until the needle is just occasionally touching the red area (or its equivalent with the flashing-lights type).
- If you and the interviewee have different levels on your voices, move the microphone closer to the weaker. Alternatively, adjust your level by talking more loudly or quietly. Don't ask your interviewee to adjust – it's off-putting.
- Make sure you have a firm yet relaxed grip on the microphone, so that you don't get tired. Hold a turn of cable between your forefinger and thumb – this will help to prevent cable bumps.
- Start recording – and keep watching those levels!

8.5 THE INTERVIEW:

Apart from avoiding questions which can be answered 'yes' or 'no', and not interrupting, and actually listening carefully to what the interviewee has to say, and all the other things good interviewers are supposed to do:

- First of all, identify yourself, your interviewee, the place, the date and the subject.
- Keep listening for extraneous noises.
- Don't move the microphone back and forth unless you absolutely have to – you'll get mic bumps unless you're very lucky.
- Keep an eye on the time – you don't want to run out of tape, and neither do you want to record 15 minutes when the brief is for 4.
- At the end, rewind and play the last few words, just to make absolutely sure the quality is satisfactory.
- Finally, label the tape clearly with your name, your interviewee's name, the date, the place and the subject.
- If you're going to record another interview, and there are only a couple of minutes left on your current reel or cassette, then wind it off in the forward direction – don't spool back. This will save your batteries. But remember to label the tape 'tail out'. And, of course, throw away the batteries so that you're forced to use new ones next time!

For more on interviewing, see Chapter 11

8.6   OUTDOOR RECORDING:

The great outdoors doesn't generally suffer from intrusive echo or reverberation. What it does have is noise. You will need to keep the microphone slightly closer to the mouth – just under the chin is a good place, so that 'popping' on plosive sounds is avoided.

The alternative is to use a directional microphone, and point the 'dead' side at the unwanted noise. This can work very well, but note that, in general, directional microphones are much more prone to popping than omnidirectional ones.

8.7   WILDTRACK RECORDING

It's often worth recording half a minute or so of the ambient sound, that is, without either you or your interviewee talking. This is particularly helpful with open-air recordings. You can then use this 'wildtrack' to cover awkward edits, and to provide a neat fade-in or out before or after some dialogue. And actuality of, for example, a cow, or a car, or whatever the subject of the interview is, will provide welcome illustration to your piece.

9 THE FLASHING BLADE: TAPE EDITING

9.1 WHY EDIT?

- To remove hesitations, repetitions, coughs etc.
- To shorten material to make it fit the limited time-slot available.
- To pick the key points out of a long and rambling interview.
- To remove errors and stumbles – 'fluffs', in the jargon.
- To add coloured leader and trailer tape at the beginning and end of a programme or insert, and to add similar spacers between the different bands of an insert tape.

9.2 TAPE EDITING EQUIPMENT

- A soft chinagraph pencil (definitely not a ball-point!).
- A sharp single-sided razor blade (take care!).
- Sticky editing-tape.
- An aluminium splicing block.

9.3 THE RULES OF TAPE EDITING

- If you can hear an edit, it's not good enough.
- Go for the easiest editing point which will give you an acceptable result.
- Always use a sharp razor blade.
- Don't discard the piece of tape you've removed until you've checked that the edit has been successful.
- Get organised. Make sure that you know what's on which reel, and that everything is clearly labelled.
- Be consistent about your cutting angle.

9.4 HOW EDITING WORKS

Editing works by deceiving the ear. You can, in principle, cut the tape anywhere you like, but it's probable that the edit will be clearly audible. What disguises the cut best of all is a good, sharp sound – a firm consonant, a door closing, a strong musical sound. What allows the edit to stick out like a sore thumb is for it to happen in the middle of so-called silence – there isn't any such thing! – or at the end of a sound, where it will cut the dying reverberation off, even in a relatively dry acoustic. So:

Where to edit:

- At the beginning of a word/sentence/paragraph.
- At the beginning of a clear noise – a clock striking, a gunshot, anything.

- On a hard consonant – t, p, b, k, etc – wherever it may fall.

For example: '...the next programme, presented by Joe Bloggs, begins in five minutes...'

- It's also possible, if you're really clever, to cut in the middle of a long sound – an sssss, perhaps.

For example: '...all the seventeen seamen were rescued safely...'

- A good, sharp intake of breath is often a strong enough place to edit.
- With coughs, ums and ers, and unwanted breaths, the same ideas always apply: look for the beginning of the sound.

Where not to edit:

- In the middle of a 'silence' or any other sort of pause. Don't be tempted – go a bit further and find the next word. Unless, of course, you're shortening a silence and can cover the edit by following it immediately with a firm sound.
- At the end of a word or sound, except when you're adding a coloured trailer tape to the end of an item or programme.

9.5 THE MECHANICS OF TAPE EDITING

The tape machine will have either two or three heads. The one you need for editing is the right-hand one – if there are three heads, this is the Playback or Replay head. If there are only two, it doubles as both Record and Replay.

- Listen to the tape, and decide where you want to make an edit.
- Play it again, and stop it at the first edit point.
- Depending on the machine you're using, you may now need to lock the tape against the head. You may need to put it into EDIT mode.

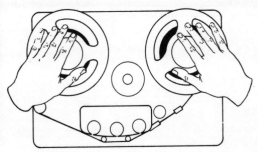

- Put one hand on each spool, and move the tape backwards and forwards until you locate the exact cutting spot. The trick is to mark just a millimetre or two before the precise sound you're aiming at, so that you don't remove anything from that sound. It's better to make short, sharp movements so that the sounds are closer to their true pitch than to low anonymous growls.
- While holding the spools stationary with one hand, mark the tape with your Chinagraph pencil exactly where it passes over the centre of the playback head.

● Find the second edit point in exactly the same way. Once again, you're looking for a point just a millimetre or two before the precise point – which is such a short time that the strong sound which follows will distract the ear from the existence of the edit.

● Pull the tape away from the head mechanism, and place it in the editing block. Line up your first mark with one of the angled cutting-grooves.

Which angle should I use?

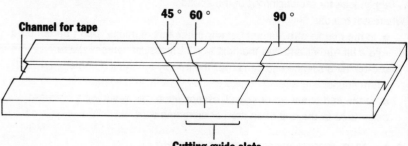

Channel for tape   **45** °   **60** °   **90** °

Cutting-guide slots

The 90-degree cut is inadvisable. It's for highly–skilled removal of clicks and pops from tape recordings of records etc.

The 45- and 60-degree cuts have little to choose between them. It's vital to be consistent, as remaking a join with two different angles is difficult. Also, it's a good idea to fall in with whatever is standard practice at your radio station.

Some people prefer 45 degrees for mono and 60 degrees for stereo. In practice, if you cut in the right place, there's little difference.

Cut the tape at the two marked points. Draw the blade through the groove at an angle, so that only the corner is blunted, not the cutting point.

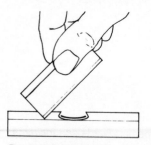

Don't throw away the removed section of tape yet!

Push the two ends of the tape together so that they just touch, with no gap and no overlap. It's best to do this away from the cutting grooves, as they can easily allow an overlap.

Cut about an inch (25mm) of sticky tape and place it carefully over the join. Make sure it's absolutely parallel to the recording tape, and none is sticking up over the edge. If it does, there's a risk of it sticking to the

pulleys and wheels when you play the tape, and the edit may be pulled apart
or the tape may just grind to a halt.

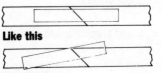

Like this

Not like this

Press the sticky tape firmly down with the tip of your finger – it's not
necessary to use fingernails.

Carefully remove the joined tape from the editing block. Don't pull it
straight up – you'll damage the edges. Give it a slight twist and it will ease
itself out safely.

Rewind the tape a few seconds and play the edited section. Be critical – if
you can hear the edit, remake it. This may mean removing a little more
tape, or putting the original piece back in and taking out a little less. It's
quite easy to take an edit apart – just fold it back along the actual joint and
it will peel apart.

9.6   PROGRAMME COMPILATION:

It's often necessary to compile a programme from different reels of original
material. Make sure everything is clearly labelled. Have one particular master
reel which starts off empty.

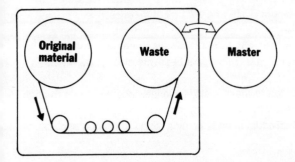

Then simply use it to replace the ordinary take-up spool each time you come to
a piece of material you really want.

9.7   LEADER AND TRAILER TAPE

This is just coloured plastic, and it cannot record sound. It's usual to use red
or red-and-white striped tape at the very end of a programme or insert tape – it
indicates to an operator that that's the end of the material. Different stations
use different colours at the beginning of a tape or in between different items –
'bands', in the jargon. Yellow is a good colour to use, as it stands out clearly.

It's vital that any leader-tape used is edited right up to the start of the following sound; if you leave a gap, then someone in a hurry lacing up your tape will play it from the end of the leader. Result: almost interminable silence!

How much to use?

● For the leader at the beginning of the tape, enough to lace up with and a bit more.

● At the end, the same, but be even more generous. It's useful to have an extra few seconds in which to stop the tape.

● In between bands, about three seconds – at 7.5 ips, that's probably roughly the width of your tape recorder!

9.8 THE LOOP

A useful editing trick is the loop. Suppose you want a certain sound effect under various links throughout your programme. You simply put several minutes of the effect onto a tape and play it in when required.

Or you can stick one end of a short length of effects tape to the other end and play it round and round on a tape machine.

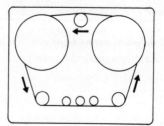

Looping the effect in this way means that it is always there; fade the sound in and out when the spirit moves you. This works best with clocks and repeated rhythmic sounds.

It's sometimes a good idea to make a slightly longer loop and run it through two adjacent tape machines. Why? The longer loop will ensure that the listener doesn't notice the same individual sounds coming round again and again.

10 THE UNIVERSAL LANGUAGE: TIME

PRINTED MATTER exists in two dimensions – along the line and down the page. Radio introduces a third dimension – time. If you're going to make programmes, you have to be able to add up and subtract, manipulate durations, make adjustments to individual items, keep a tally of how things are going, and remember the vital rule:

Start on time and end on time and it doesn't really matter what happens in between!

The key concept is the fixed point. This might be an hourly news bulletin shared with other stations, which therefore must start exactly on time. Or a time signal, which waits for no-one. Or the constraint may be that the following programme is pre-recorded, of known duration, and must not overrun – therefore it can't start late, and our programme must end in good time.

Different networks adopt different policies. BBC Radio Three has very few fixed points, while most commercial stations have hourly bulletins from a central news service. And BBC World Service has even more fixed points to allow for the frequent transmitter changes which short-wave broadcasting demands, and also for the requirements of rebroadcasters.

10.1 TALK TIMING

Everyone talks at a different speed. Three words to the second, or 180 to the minute, is a reasonable average, but pacey presentation will be quicker, while more considered programmes will be slower. So time yourself on a stopwatch, count the number of words, divide the two numbers and work out your own speed. It may be more useful to work out your personal number of lines per minute – you can then add up quickly the likely duration of a magazine programme linking script, for example. It's likely to be about 12 to 20 lines per minute.

10.2 MAGAZINE TIMING

You've got a half-hour live slot to fill. You have 8 items. That means that by the time you've taken off the signature tune (or sting), menu and closing announcement, there's probably only about 3'30" per item:

Overall duration	30'00"
Signature tune	20"
Opening announcement	10"
Menu	30"

Closing announcement	30"
Closing signature tune	30"
Time left for items	28'00"

And this 3'30" must include the link preceding the item! So how do you make sure you don't fall behind or sprint ahead of the schedule? There's a system called back-timing...

10.3   BACK-TIMING

This system means that, as well as adding up the individual durations of the items in your programme so that you know in overall terms whether you have too much or too little material, you also perform a different sort of calculation.

What you do is to work backwards from the required end-time of the programme.

So:

Must end at		12.30'00"
Closing signature tune	30"	must start at 12.29'30"
Closing announcement	30"	must start at 12.29'00"
Last item	3'00"	must start at 12.26'00"
Intro to last item	30"	must start at 12.25'30"
Previous item	2'45"	must start at 12.22'45"
Intro to previous item	20"	must start at 12.22'25"

...and so on back through the programme. Now, if you've got the right overall duration of items and linking script and signature tunes, then the start-time you need in order to come out on time will be the same as the start-time you've been allocated by whoever runs the station or network.

However, back in the real world, it's extremely unlikely that you'll be so lucky.

So what you do is this: you make any radical changes to your contents, cutting 20 seconds here and adding 30 seconds there, so that the whole thing is approximately right. Then you note any other places where you can easily add or subtract – if you're a bit short, why not let that live interview run on for another half minute? Finally, you mark up the master copy of your script with the time that each segment must begin.

Then, once you get on the air and the programme is happening all around you, you check how far adrift you are at each point. If you're a few seconds late, ask your presenter to speed up, or trim a bit out of one of the later items. If you're a bit early, ask your presenter to slow down a little, or add a few words, or play a little more of that record that illustrates an item.

Just keep checking the clock at every junction between items, and you'll come out accurately at the end of the show.

11 WHY ALL THE QUESTIONS? THE ART OF THE INTERVIEW

QUESTIONS are seeking answers. Answers are information. The radio interviewer is trying to elicit information from an interviewee for the benefit of the listener. The radio interview is just one way of transferring information.

11.1 USING AND ABUSING INTERVIEW TECHNIQUE

Although the radio interview usually involves two people, there are exceptions. At news conferences many interviewers are invited to throw questions at a single respondent. This is a useful device for controlling a group of journalists and preventing any one line of questioning from going too far. A single interviewer may question several members of a successful sports team. This is more amusing on television than on radio, as bored, sweaty losers await their turn to be sick as a parrot. All too often, discussion programmes are reduced to multilateral interviews by inept chairpersons who staunch the flow of argument with intrusive questioning.

11.2 INTERVIEWS v. TALKS

The interview has some advantages over the straight talk:

First there is variety of sound. There are not too many voices that can hold a listener's attention for three minutes. Breaking the flow with a second voice helps to hold the listener's attention.

Second, it is easier for an interviewee to answer intelligent questions than to write a talk. On the other hand, the devising of intelligent questions makes the job of interviewer quite difficult.

In some cases, the interviewer is also the programme presenter. This is certainly true of most current-affairs magazine programmes. On national networks the presenter/interviewer will have the support of a producer: in local radio he or she will be self-sufficient in every sense. But while presenters are encouraged to interview, they are discouraged from doing talks for their own programmes.

11.3 THE PROCESS

The process that goes to produce the final on-air interview is more complicated than you would imagine.

In the beginning is The Idea. Ideas come from many sources but in the case of current affairs they probably derive from news.

11.4 RESEARCH

Does the idea lend itself to the interview format? You get less information per minute from an interview than from a straight talk where the words are under control.

Having had your idea you will need to research the subject in order to develop a line of questioning. Chatting with the office know-all is not real research. Uncorroborated assertions on controversial subjects are a shaky foundation.

Try delving through archives or newspaper cuttings. Telephone conversations with acknowledged authorities on the subject help. As with all sources, it is useful to have more than one.

11.5 ANGLE

Another name for a line of questioning is an 'angle'. Your interview will only last a few minutes. The narrower its scope, the more searching it can be. Tomorrow is another day. The listener does not expect the secrets of the cosmos in three minutes.

11.6 VICTIM

Part of your research concerns the choice of a 'victim'. Broadcasters depend on a contacts book. Under subject-headings there are names, titles, telephone numbers (office and home) and addresses. There may even be notes about the performer's abilities in front of the microphone.

Ring early. You are not alone in the market. Your idea is unlikely to be original and the best specialists are snapped up fast. If your first choice is unavailable, have other numbers to ring.

No sooner have you booked the third name on your list, a prolix performer with a marked stammer, than your first choice rings through to announce his availability.

If you have doubts about an interviewee then you should hedge your bets when you call:

'We're thinking of doing a two-way about Catholicism in Ruritania. Would you be interested, if the editor decides to go ahead?'

Better a little diplomacy than disentangling a premature commitment.

Your conversation with your interviewee is designed to cover the ground without going into specific questions and answers.

If the interviewee is new to you then a preliminary conversation reveals a lot about quality of voice, articulateness, speech velocity and subject knowledge.

11.7 PREPARING QUESTIONS

Resist the temptation to write down your questions. Pre-arranged questions often sound inappropriate as the answers deviate from the expected course. In a pre-recorded interview you only know one question: the first. In a 'live' interview, you and your victim may pre-arrange two questions, the first and the last.

You must allow questions to develop organically from the interview itself. Listen to what is being said. Genuine curiosity coupled with your research should provide you with enough interrogatory ammunition. Remember – you are asking questions on behalf of the listener.

11.8   VISUALS

For an interviewee there is nothing so uncommunicative as the top of an interviewer's head. The eyes have it. Look at the person speaking. You will learn to express interest and empathy without uttering a word.

11.9   SHOWING OFF

In spite of all that research, resist the temptation to display your knowledge. The listener is prepared to take it for granted. The person the listener wishes to hear is the interviewee, not the interviewer. Without being perfunctory, keep your questions to the point. In a three-minute interview, three thirty-second questions is approaching the greedy.

Experts do not make the best interviewers. They are too tempted to display their own prejudices, involving the interviewee in a detailed, professional discussion which leaves the listener floundering in their wake.

11.10   IS THIS A GOOD QUESTION?

What kind of questions produce answers? Certainly not the kind of questions that can produce the answer 'yes' or 'no'. Start your questions with words such as 'what', 'when', 'who', 'where', 'how' or 'why'. These are sure to produce longer, more informative answers.

11.11   CATEGORIES OF INTERVIEW

There are two basic types of interview. The majority fall into a category we call 'conspiracy interviews'. There's nothing sinister about the term. It simply suggests that two people agree or 'conspire' to pass the information one of them possesses to listeners via responses to questions. There is concord.

'Confrontational Interviews', on the other hand, are between people who are not in agreement as to the nature of the information to be passed to the listener. The political interview tends to fall into this category.

The politician is far from reluctant to communicate with the listener. He wishes to communicate a message of his own, not necessarily connected to your questions. The fundamental media assumption that certain politicians are parsimonious with the truth is not ill-founded. It is the interviewer's job to extract a little more of that reluctant commodity.

11.12   DEMEANOUR

Once in the studio, you will have other things to consider. You are the host and your job, whatever you may think of the guest, is to be welcoming. If you are nervous or distracted, this will convey itself to the victim.

Beware of sheets of paper. Even professional broadcasters like to make a few notes about subjects to be raised in the interview. Paper rustles. It offers a counter-attraction to the interviewee's eyes.

11.13   PROS

Professional interviewees abound. They browse in the groves of academe or arcadia, waiting for the call. Such people rely on radio for a useful addition to their income. Such people will meet you half way. They want to know how long you want and pride themselves on achieving your required duration.

The pre-recorded interview tends to be longer than required. Editing can solve any problems of length. There's time for re-takes. If there's a producer sitting in the cubicle, timings will be kept, suggestions made, whole interviews re-done.

'Live' interviews are something else. They must run to time. That is the reason for the pre-arranged, final question. This is something very specific. 'When will you be bringing the show back to London?' Answer: 'In February.'

It is good sense to let your interviewee know about that question in advance. Then you both know that time is up. It may not seem like ethical practice but it avoids all those warning phrases that interviewers deploy in a desperate attempt to shut their victim up.

'Well, finally and in a few words because we're running out of time, what is your view of the universe?'

Knowing the time is important. If you are going to crash a commercial, very important. Studios have clocks. Producers and studio managers have clocks. By pre-arrangement they can show you a green light when there is a minute left of your three, another green at thirty seconds and leave the light glowing with only fifteen seconds to go.

If you wish to indicate to your interviewee that he should bring his answer to a rapid close, do so with an agreed signal. A trembling finger poking in the air is inadequate when you have ten seconds left to run.

11.14   ...AND FINALLY!

One other point. Radiophonic sympathy. If your interviewee has a gentle manner, restrain your confident enthusiasm. Your rounded, professional tones will only sound arrogant and overbearing. You must not risk losing the sympathy of the listener.

12 GIFT OF THE GAB: WRITING FOR RADIO

'SAY IT Before You Write It.' That's the only cardinal rule of talks writing for radio. The good radio talk must live up to its name. It is neither literature nor print journalism. It is made with the mouth.

12.1 SPEECH PATTERNS
Speech has very different patterns from the silent written word. The syntax is simpler. For example, there are fewer subordinate clauses. Broken phrases, sentences without verbs, even noises, are permissible in the radio talk.

12.2 ELISION
One of the fundamental distinctions between written and spoken English is the practice of elision. 'We do not say' is something we don't say. In the formal essay, on the other hand, we do not write 'we don't write.'

12.3 DICTION
Diction is not just another word for enunciation. It can also refer to the choice of vocabulary and syntax. There is a level of diction appropriate to everyday speech that would horrify the silent writer. Slang, ephemeral words, clichés; all find their place in the talk. But good radio-talks writers fully comprehend that there are certain collocations which they must eschew at all costs!

12.4 SPOT THE HIDDEN TRAPS
Saying your words aloud before writing them helps in more ways than one. Not only can you hear how it sounds, you'll also find out whether you can handle the material vocally, without stumbling over difficult expressions or running out of breath at the wrong moment, the way some people do who have a tendency to compose sentences beyond the lung capacity of even the greatest of Shakespearian actors. Giving tongue to your words also means that tongue-twisters and unintentional puns will come out of the closet.

12.5 THE SINGULAR AUDIENCE
Remember the paradox: although the audience may number millions you address them in the second person singular.

Imagine a friend sitting beyond your microphone, listening with interest to what you're saying. That is your audience. It's the same audience I'm imagining as I write these words. In the case of a book, the single reader is an appropriate image; in radio, a mass medium, it's more difficult to hold such an image in your mind. Since the audience is one person, do not lecture, hector or preach.

12.6 TALKS v. LECTURES

Talks are often referred to as 'straight pieces'. The name is suggested by the fact that a talk is delivered straight through without a break. But this doesn't mean you have to be 'straight' in every way. Formal public lectures often begin with an introduction, outlining what the lecture will contain. The argument is then developed and a conclusion arrived at. You might call this the A to Z method.

University lectures are delivered to a group of more or less enthusiastic listeners who have chosen to attend them. Your audience of one may not have switched on with the specific intention of listening to your talk.

12.7 OPENERS

Imagine you are the speaker invited to amuse the radio audience during the interval of a promenade concert. Your have thirty seconds to convince your listener that your talk is preferable to the refreshing cup that cheers. Will your words intrigue or drive your audience from the room?

'Showing off was an accepted part of a musician's life in eighteenth century Rome. The Scarlatti family were particularly good at it. Il padre would sit at the harpsichord and invent a melody. Il figlio would then take Father's place and improvise on the tune. The assembled audience of Roman aristocrats would show their approval. Whereupon Scarlatti senior would improvise on his son's improvisations to even more enthusiastic applause. Well, one day...'

Radio 3 listeners might be surprised at such a 'populist' opening to a talk but Promenade Concerts attract a far wider audience than that network's usual aficionados.

12.8 CONTENT

Notice something else. The talk uses two simple Italian expressions. The device of introducing these words flatters by assuming knowledge. At the same time, contextual translations are offered which do not insult the ignorant.

Why bother to depart from English? A student used this device brilliantly in a talk about a trip through South America. Throughout the talk, she scattered Spanish expressions whose meaning was perfectly clear from the context. We were transported to another country and her story gained both colour and verisimilitude.

12.9 SURPRISE, SURPRISE

Without straining the listener's credulity too far, try for obliquity. Or at least, avoid the obvious.

'I wonder what happened to my local nuclear power station? It was there only yesterday, blocking my mind like a bad dream.'

...may prove rather more stimulating than:

'Nuclear power in Britain seems to be a spent force, with the decision by the government to exclude...'

12.10 THE NUMBERS GAME

What should you avoid in a radio talk? One million eight hundred and seventy-nine thousand four hundred and twenty-one.

The ear is not the most reliable conduit of factual information. Think of the childhood game of Chinese whispers. A group of ten people sit in a circle. The first person whispers a message in a neighbour's ear. The message is passed around the circle and arrives at its place of origin garbled beyond recognition.

Complicated numbers are indigestible. If statistics have to be used, round them off. Rather than 1,879,421 try 'nearly two million'. It has a better chance of lodging in the brain.

Too many facts lead to mental constipation on radio. Unlike the reader of a newspaper, the listener cannot turn back the page to check a fact or figure.

12.11 THE TALKS MARKET

The radio talk may be a weather report or a letter from America. Anything, from the shortest of trails for a programme to the most learned of disquisitions comes under the heading. It's rare for a general broadcaster to be asked to write talks. If this radio form is your particular bent then study the market.

Once you have found a programme which uses straight pieces, listen to it scientifically. What is the programme trying to do? What is the level of diction? Colloquial? Formal? How long are the pieces? Are the talks delivered by the same 'resident' people? Do they only invite specialists? If you are a freelance, programmes are the market and you will need to study them thoroughly. Often you will only have one chance to submit a piece. Make sure it works.

Naturally, none of the above needs apply to the genius. Such a person will be above the petty rules of radio.

Radio and the talk are both evolving. There is no absolute standard of what constitutes the good radio talk. Fashions change and you could be the person who sets a new one.

12.12 UNTO YOURSELF BE TRUE...

Another student chose childbirth as the subject of the first radio talk she had ever written. Tearing the veil off the fictions that surround having a child by contrasting reality with romance, she had the course members rocking with laughter. Using humour to drive home a subcutaneous message takes real talent.

Technique will only take you so far. Truth to life is just as important. Writing about something you know or care about helps convince the listener.

12.13 OTHER KINDS OF WRITING

There are those within the profession whose business is writing talks material, particularly in Presentation and in News.

Presentation is selling. Trails tend to use 'hot' writing, seeking to persuade. News persuades by its coolness, its unemotional, detached quality.

The writer of a programme trail will exert every verbal muscle to convince you that what is being 'sold' is unmissable. The news-writer or the correspondent filing a despatch uses a different diction, avoiding emotive words and exciting aural punctuation. News has no exclamation marks!

What happens to that brilliant script after you have written it? What about speaking your words in front of the microphone? There are some techniques that will help you deliver your talk, once it is written. You will find them in the next section.

13 MOUTH MUSIC: THE ART OF PRESENTATION

PRESENTATION is, above all, the art of disguising art. The human voice tells us many things. We think we can recognise personality and character by shutting our eyes and listening to another speak. So as a radio presenter, it is your job to analyse those preconceptions and use them to your advantage.

13.1 WARMTH

It doesn't matter whether you are reading an obituary or presenting a disc show, the listener responds to warmth. Warmth suggests sympathy, welcome, friendliness.

13.2 AUTHORITY

An equally important attribute of good presentation is authority. This is not confined to 'serious' subjects, such as news or current affairs, classical music or learned talks. Even DJ's need to sound totally on top of their subject, otherwise they lack credibility. Authority is a combination of confidence and accuracy, particularly in terms of pronunciation.

13.3 MUSICALITY

You might think this isn't too important a quality but a musical voice seduces the listener into absorbing your message. Geoffrey Weekes, one of the finest presenters I ever heard, used to exhort, 'Use your voice as an instrument - play tunes on it.'

13.4 VOCAL RANGE

The speaking voice has a relatively small range. Most people do not even make full use of that. Monotony may be normal but it doesn't make good radio, unless you want people to switch off or fall asleep.

13.5 EGO

To be a good presenter you need a healthy dose of egotism. You may not love your voice but you must act as though you do, so that it is worthy of the medium.

Examine your vocal disabilities with a cold, professional ear. Do I lack clarity? Am I gabbling? Is my voice too thin? Do I have a problem with sibilance? Professionals can train you to speak well but in the end it depends on practice. Find yourself a tape-recorder and read something, anything, into it. Listen to the result. Try again, modifying the voice, experimenting.

13.6 DEEP BREATHING

Breathing is often a problem with presenters. Not everybody can deliver Shakespearian soliloquies in one breath. So when you write your material, follow the golden rule. 'Say it before you write it'. Only then will you be sure that your lungs and diaphragm can cope.

13.7 NOISES ON

There is one school of presentation which believes that radio demands a range of noises which would cause embarrassment in real life, namely, lip-smacking, exhalations, inhalations and clicks of all sorts. Any station with a 'compressor-limiter' on the transmitter makes audible breathing sound like an advanced case of emphysema.

13.8 MEANING

No matter how beautiful the voice, nothing will reach the listener's inner ear unless you make sense. The primary task of a presenter is to understand the primary meaning of the material. Oddly enough, even people who write their own scripts do not always know how to 'lift it off the page'.

13.9 MARKS

There is a system of marks that can help you find your way through a script.

For new presenters, all scripts are difficult. And even the most experienced presenters may experience a 'dry'; that horrible moment when they realise they are sitting in a studio talking to millions of listeners and the brain shuts down in panic. Marking the script may help you get through a blackout.

Everybody develops their own system of marking scripts; here are a few suggestions.

● Underlining: this is the standard technique for marking an emphasis. But there are variations on the theme. A single line may be doubled or trebled for greater emphasis. This does not necessarily mean doubling or trebling the volume of the voice. Emphasis is a relative thing. For some situations it is better to slow down on a key word – especially a difficult name, a title or an unusual term – and this is marked by a broken underlining.

● Diagonals: silence is eloquent. And the length of a pause is important. Pauses are punctuation. A short pause (a single diagonal line) marks a full stop, a longer one (a double diagonal) a paragraph.

● Up and Down: some presenters even mark when the voice will rise and fall. Again, the movement of the voice denotes the punctuation, the voice rising at a comma (marked by a rising arrow) and falling at a full stop (a dipping arrow). This fall of the voice is called a cadence.

Remember that you alone have the script. The listener is relying on your voice and its inflections to indicate where the punctuation marks lie.

13.10 PACE V SPEED

Pace is a curious concept. It is often confused with speed. Speed is an average concept. (He reads at a 120 words a minute). For the purposes of this course, pace means variations in speed.

It's always advisable to begin reading a talk slightly more slowly. This gives the listener time to adjust to the sound of your voice. Once the ear is tuned in, half-way through the first sentence, you can move into your normal speed. Similarly, it is a convention of radio that a presenter will slow down on the very last words of a talk.

Do not read too evenly. Those who are unsure tend to emphasise too many words in a sentence, or, worse, stress the wrong words such as articles or prepositions ('a', 'the', 'to', 'on'). When looking for primary meaning, you will find no more than two or three words in each sentence that require emphasis. These are the key words. The rest are in a real sense linguistic padding. Your pace can increase for padding.

13.11 CLICHÉS

Speech consists of groups of words, collocations, rather than strings of single words. Every human being has a head full of clichés, groups of words which are produced as required. For expressing our basic needs quickly, clichés are all-important. Unusual words will only slow down the process of assimilation of the information. This explains why so much news and current affairs is predictable and cliché-rridden. But in every cliché there is a word (or two) which is important to the message. Discriminate with pace between the important and the less important.

13.12 PRONUNCIATION

If you are really keen to lose credibility, mispronounce someone's name. You will give the impression that you just don't know or care about your subject.

The one rule is: check everything!

There are pronouncing dictionaries available, and your station may well have a policy for words with more than one option.

- Use established anglicisations – Paris with a final s, and not as the French say it.
- Use English sounds which are close to the original – if you slip into a true German pronunciation of a particular word, then the change from English to German and back again will throw your rhythm, at least, and your talk will become less comprehensible.
- Use whatever pronunciation you are most natural with for English words – Newcastle with a short a if that's what you normally say. But if you normally use a long, southern English a, then stick to that – otherwise you will sound as if you are making fun of Northerners.
- If you don't know how to pronounce something, and there's no time to

check, stress all syllables equally. This will provide the least bad outcome.

● Mark up your script with the key stresses and any other pronunciation details. This is one of the reasons for a double-spaced script – there's more room for such notes.

A good test: Take an article from a newspaper. Read it, mark it and record it. Play it back to your friends and then ask them questions about the content. The better the presentation, the smarter they will seem.

14 BUT PERFECTLY FORMED: THE ART OF THE PACKAGE

THE EDITOR of a British satirical magazine once described a friendly rival as 'small but perfectly formed'. The package for radio should answer to the same description.

In different parts of the world the package has been described as a 'mini-doc' (mini-documentary) or as a 'featurette'. (When you read the chapter on documentaries and features you will realise the derivation of the junior titles). The term 'package' avoids all kinds of misunderstandings.

14.1 WHAT?

The package embraces, within a few minutes, almost any combination of radiophonic elements you may wish. The most usual formula contains edited elements of interviews, actuality and linking scripted passages.

14.2 WHY?

Packages live in the world of the magazine programme. You are already familiar with the interview and the talk (or 'straight piece'). The package includes elements of both.

There are subjects on radio that cry out for more than the simple studio piece with its clean acoustics. The package can re-create a sense of real life by using the skills of the interviewer, the writer, the tape editor and the reporter to bring the outside world to the listener. The package colours a black and white radio picture.

14.3 HOW?

There are numerous ways to assemble a package. The classic method uses the services of a reporter who assembles inserts of original interviews and location recordings (actuality). The reporter is also expected to write a linking script and voice it.

There is another kind of current-affairs package that requires great skill in re-assembling pre-recorded material. Here's a hypothetical example: the release of a hostage evokes comment from the Secretary General of the United Nations, the President of the United States, the hostage, the hostage's wife, his friends, and so on. The material has already been broadcast as separate items earlier in the day.

This kind of package is called a 'pull-together'. The compiler of such a package needs to be able to select the most relevant extracts, edit tape efficiently and be able to write a solid script. Speed may also be a consideration.

In current-affairs magazines the package has a further important function. A reporter is sent out to investigate a controversial issue; for example, miners and their wives, local trades-unionists and mine managers giving their views on the closure of the last local pit. Of course, in a short package the reporter can only hope to summarise the contending views. But the good 'report' can serve as a useful prelude to a studio debate between the President of the Union and the Minister for Energy.

Yet another type of package relates to the 'issue' report. Suppose that neither the President of the Union nor the Minister for Energy wishes to take part in a debate about the last local pit. You can, however, create a debate by interviewing both individuals separately and intercutting their answers. To be scrupulously fair you will have to put the same questions to both. You don't need their permission to do the piece this way but you should let them know that it is your intention. Their right is to decline to take part.

Not all packages involve location work. Some may be assembled in the studio without actuality of any description. Historical or arts subjects may only require a mixture of music, professional voices reading written extracts and a good linking script.

There is an odd-man-out in the world of the package – the linked interview. This is an interview from which the questions have been excised and replaced by linking script. This technique gives rise to suspicions about the original interview. Were the questions ineffectual? Was the sound irremediably unbalanced? Clearly, how the listener responds to the final, broadcast piece is all that matters, but for a busy programme the time wasted in re-packaging a simple interview is not going to endear the perpetrator to the editor.

14.4   HOW LONG?

The variety of elements found in a package means that the ear is refreshed. The greater complexity of a package may mean a longer time on the air. In a thirty-minute magazine programme, where interviews run to around three minutes and talks to two, packages will run to between four and six minutes. The longer the programme, the longer the package it can carry. But in those parts of the radio world enamoured of the sound-bite, packages tend to shrink accordingly.

14.5   ACTION POINTS

Once you know the range of elements included in the package, you will have a fair idea of how to go about making one.

- In the beginning is the Idea. Whether yours or somebody else's, it must lend itself to this kind of treatment.
- Next comes the research, the telephoning of potential contributors, the making of appointments, the booking of studios. Never underestimate how

long it will take to move from one interview to another. Leave plenty of margin for error.

● If location recording is needed, then you must make sure that the portable tape recorder is booked. If the equipment is your own, make sure it is fit for the job. Take spare batteries and tapes with you.

● Travel means transport. It's your job to arrive at appointments on time. Excuses, no matter how genuine, always sound ineffectual. Angry contributors may even leave you in the lurch.

● Take your information with you. Telephone numbers are of no use in an office drawer if you are running late for an important appointment.

● Identify all your material, not only by labelling all tapes (take a pen), but with your voice on the tape itself. This will help at the editing stage.

● Ensure that all recordings are checked before you leave any location. Contributors won't mind doing an interview twice if you are professional enough to notice an error immediately.

● If you used a cassette recorder, make sure the recordings are transferred to quarter-inch tape for editing. Annotate and time all your material. This process will suggest which material cannot be used, even if at this stage you are unsure about what can.

● Edit your tapes. The usual ratio of inserts to script is two or three to one. A six-minute package will need about four-minutes' worth of material. This means being harsh on your own material. All package makers over-record.

● Once you have an assembled tape of inserts, you can begin to write your linking script. The aggregate time of the inserts indicate how much script you need.

● If you require any additional material, such as recorded music or effects, now is the time to listen to them and time the sections you need.

● You may find that before you record your piece, a producer or editor will wish to read the script and listen to the inserts. Type your script with clear technical instructions. Do not use paper that is likely to rustle in front of the microphone.

● Record your piece. The producer or editor may invite you to re-record some of your links. It may be part of your job to edit the re-takes into the piece.

● Before handing the final package over, make sure you have listened to the edited version and timed it.

● Give the editor details of any contributors who need paying. Payment must be by pre-arrangement. Do not agree to pay without permission from the station.

● With your tape hand over a written cue or introduction to the piece. Do not be offended if the presenter re-writes it.

● If you have them, submit details of expenses. Give the editor details of any recorded material covered by copyright agreements.

● If necessary, write your letters of thanks.

● If you are a freelance, wait as patiently as you can for your fee.

As you see, the package takes time and trouble; more time and trouble than a busy magazine-producer can afford. It's not unknown for people on the staff of radio stations to make packages but in Britain this activity is the especial province of the freelance.

The freelance becomes adept at balancing the cost and reward of any particular job. Packages may receive better payment than interviews or talks but there comes a point beyond which they become uneconomic.

The easiest packages involve one nearby location, good sound possibilities, eager interviewees and a simple subject. Even so, this package is likely to take a day and a half to do. Half a day to record the material, half a day to edit, half a day to script and put together in the the studio.

Packages which demand longer time and more difficulty can earn greater rewards but there is a clear limit to what a producer will pay for a six-minute segment of a thirty-minute programme. The relationship of reward to effort means that the freelance package is not the best place for investigative journalism. Freelances themselves sniff at jobs that demand too much time checking. Payment relates to time on air, not time in pre-production.

An exciting package can add immeasurably to the attractions of a studio-bound magazine programme but this must be weighed against the cost in resources.

The package can also be dangerous. Contributors to radio whose words can affect their futures, such as politicians or businessmen, need to get across their message in as unadulterated a fashion as possible. This is why they prefer a three-minute live interview to thirty seconds in your package.

The principles which govern the making of a package are the same as those relating to all news and current affairs broadcasting. The editing blade gives you wonderful opportunities to shape the material. That shaping must remain true to the code of practice and to what you know your victims meant.

All programme material relating to controversial issues creates difficulties for the broadcaster but if you can justify your package according to the principles of fair conduct then you have nothing to fear.

15 THE VOX POP

WHILE one kind of package may demand great skill in interviewing; and another, ingenious script-writing; a third requires the resilience of a door-to-door salesman and the flashing blade of a D'Artagnan.

The vox pop, short for vox populi (the voice of the people), is such a peculiar package that we have decided to give it a small chapter of its own.

15.1 ALL YOU SURVEY

There is a fascination in finding out what people think. Not just individuals but groups. Pollsters checking public opinion of political parties are the bane of the parliamentarian's life. Pressure groups seek to find out how many members of the public support their causes. The numbers game is part of the democratic process. Nobody disputes that. What is in dispute is how prominent a part numbers should play.

15.2 THE RADIO VERSION

Radio can also join in the game with a less ambitious variation on the survey. Gathering twenty opinions on the latest tax measure hardly constitutes a true reflection of public opinion. But the vox pop can be instructive as well as sheer fun.

Uninstructed public opinion only goes so far on radio. A vox pop may be allowed to run for no longer than a minute as part of a package or a documentary or as the introduction to another item on the same subject.

15.3 WHERE DOES RESILIENCE COME IN?

Imagine our hardy interviewer, stationed in front of a large store in London's Oxford Street. A potential victim is approached.

'Excuse me. I'm from the BBC World Service and we're putting together a programme about the cost of Christmas. May I ask you a question or two?'

The faintest of nods from the victim. A few other pedestrians cluster out of curiosity. The interviewer flicks a switch on his machine.

'What are you going to buy for your family this Christmas?'

The interviewee frowns, shakes his head and pushes his way through the crowd of media watchers. All the red-faced interviewer records is their collective snigger. That is where resilience comes in.

15.4 ACTION POINTS

- Decide whether the subject lends itself to this format. Belief in the after-life may not be best dealt with by a vox pop on a street corner.
- Choose the most appropriate question/s to ask. There will probably be only one and you must put it to everybody in the same way if the survey is to have any meaning.
- Decide on the appropriate location. You need a place frequented by many people. You want atmosphere that is not too intrusive. The public house is a tempting location; lots of people and ambience. Don't be tempted: the crowded bar has too much of both for bearable radio. Locations will suggest themselves. Instead of waiting for your quarry to cross your path, you may have to visit an institution such as a school or a hospital.
- Make sure your portable recorder is in good shape. If you need the piece quickly, a quarter-inch machine is heavier but more convenient for rapid editing. You won't need too many spare tapes but spare batteries are always a good idea.
- Set your machine on 'play', 'record' and 'pause'. The recording level should be such that you can place the microphone close to the victim's mouth. This will help to reduce background noise.
- When you approach someone always introduce yourself with your name and the identity of your station. If the person stops, explain what you are doing and why. Do not be dismayed if people refuse to co-operate. It's their right. There's no need to be importunate.
- If the person agrees, try to get some kind of level without running the tape. With the recorder set as described above, you will be able to see the needle or L.E.Ds indicate level.
- As the question is the same for all respondents there is no need to record it each time. Ask the question, then flick off the pause switch. You will collect a series of answers.
- Beware of background noise. If you are in any doubts about the volume of sound coming from a passing bus or plane, ask the interviewee if you can put the question again. Most people will respect your professionalism if you explain your reason for re-recording.
- Even quite low noises may sound odd in the final edited version if they end too abruptly. Think ahead to the next stage.
- There is no perfect number of interviews to collect for a vox pop. Nor can you set a definite time-limit on the operation. It's not enough to return after an hour with seven unusable comments.
- Even though you have an adequate number of usable answers, if your deadline permits, persist until you record an answer which tingles your spine. That is the cherry on the cake.
- You will have recognised the final quote of your vox pop the moment you recorded it. It may be your cherry.

● Listen to your tape and time the inserts, annotating as you go. A simple system of ticks (for possible) and crosses (for impossible) is usually enough. Do not be tempted by remarks that need five plays to understand. Comprehensibility is all.

● Balance your answers between male and female, light and dark voices. Do not be satisfied if things are merely satisfactory. The art of the vox pop is the art of juxtaposition. While each answer has its own meaning, a whole new dimension is added by the creative ordering of the answers.

● Sometimes you can try interpolation, inserting a negative comment between two halves of another answer. Every sound is grist to the vox pop mill – giggles, snorts of derision, even abuse. Waste not, want not.

● If possible, build to a climax. Do not end your vox pop on a weak note, unless you are deliberately seeking amusement through the device of anti-climax.

15.5 CAVEAT

Although the vox pop is not the most profound of radio forms, it must be treated with professional respect. Even though your respondents are anonymous, they may ask you for the time of broadcast of your programme. They may listen. Having fun at their expense is acceptable; making them sound ridiculous is another. The flashing blade must be used honourably on the defenceless victims of radio.

16 BITS AND PIECES: MAGAZINE PROGRAMMES

MAGAZINE PROGRAMMES are mixed bags. On the BBC's Radio 4, the 'Today' programme has as mixed a bag of items as you could wish: religious talks, press reviews, weather reports, time checks, road reports, sport, financial news, packages, live discussions, repartee between presenters, the odd musical item and dozens of interviews. Magazine programmes don't have to be quite as varied as that. Their range can be quite narrow, in fact. Motoring magazines, for example, are likely to contain road tests, product reports, items about the law, discussions about lubricants or seat belts. There are magazine programmes for women, the consumer, the disabled, the old and the young; think of a special interest and there's bound to be a magazine about it somewhere. Magazines can change their moods, like the publications from which they take their name. A standard modulation is from the serious 'lead' item through to a final 'funny'. Conventionally, jokes are only tolerated as tail-pieces.

16.1 HORS D'OEUVRES
The first thing that appears on a magazine programme is an introduction. This may be a voice or music or both, in other words a 'voice-over'. Signature tunes stir up tumultuous emotions in radio. At one end of the spectrum are those who must have music wherever they go; at the other, those who think a simple 'hello' is all that a magazine requires. I must confess to a weakness for a sense of theatre and that is what the signature-tune suggests to me.

But not at any price. Music must be right. Producers can spend hours searching for the signature- tune of their dreams, or may even commission a composer for something special and all for about twenty seconds of air time. After that the listener becomes restless, waiting for the sound of a voice. Music, when it fades, must fade naturally, on a cadence and not in the middle of a phrase.

A new technique with opening music is to incorporate a voiced-over announcement of the programme title followed by a repeated phrase of music. Over this a menu or news-headlines may be read. Once the menu or headlines are over a second piece of music crashes in as a full stop.

Or you may decide on that simple 'hello'.

Whatever you decide, your next decision concerns the menu.

16.2 MENUS
Menus are either too long or too short. They usually follow a formula.

'Hello, this is Michael Kaye welcoming you to another edition of Stop-Gap
and in today's edition...
The automatic house of the future...
Why all mothers-in-law do it...
And sausages that bite back...
But first, Margaret Thatcher's decision to join the Labour Party...'
Familiar? This is the menu disguised as a series of teasers. The teaser is a
useful device to intrigue and persuade the listener to stay tuned. Your first
thirty seconds are all you have. If your listener is not intrigued by then, the dial
will be turned to another station. Don't be too smart but please avoid the
dogged menu.

'Hello, this is Michael Kaye with another edition of Stop-Gap, our weekly
thirty-minute magazine programme for all those items that won't fit anywhere
else...
In today's programme...The Japanese design for a computer-driven house
where all the house work is done by machines...
The habit that mothers-in-law have of offering unwanted advice to their
daughters about grandchildren...
And the new kind of sausage full of spices which will burn your mouth if
you're not careful...
But we begin with the announcement in this morning's Guardian newspaper,
since denied by Mrs. Thatcher herself...'
The second menu is not wrong. It just gives too much of the game away.
The description of the first item is so complete that there is almost no need to
listen to the programme. The same almost applies to the other items. Perhaps
a judicious balance between the titillating and the prosaic is what is needed.

Whatever style you hit upon, remember the presenter must write it. There is
no virtue in hiring only the voice beautiful. Voices are most convincing when
they read their own words. Also, remember that the listener wants to get on
with the programme, not just listen to a menu.

In fact, it would be no bad thing in a long programme to select just a very
few of the best items or even dispense with a menu altogether. There are
presenters who feel they must talk about everything on the programme and
whose introduction and menu may drag on for two minutes. If you spend more
than a minute (including sig tune) getting to the first cue, then you are testing
the listener's patience and memory.

16.3   INGREDIENTS

When deciding on the content of a magazine programme, producers draw their
ideas from a wide variety of sources. Sadly, newspapers and printed
magazines are still a major fount. As radio develops its own reporters and
correspondents, fewer clues will be sought in the national press. But too many
radio people bury their heads in newspapers when they reach the office.

Then there is spontaneous generation of ideas. This is the province of the novice producer who has always wanted to go to prison... (to find out what it feels like, you understand)... and will use any excuse to wangle a visit to one with a tape-recorder.

There is no point in recalling that the last fourteen producers each did the same thing within weeks of joining the programme. Enthusiasm must be given full rein. After all, somebody out there may not have heard the previous fourteen items. And, who knows? Number fifteen may turn out to be brilliant.

16.4   CHEFS

Specialist magazine producers tend to develop a network of people in their area and make a note of their names, addresses (for payment), their telephone numbers (home and office) and vocal accomplishments (articulate, light voice).

The danger with such a network is that it may become what is known as a stage army, the same old voices on the same old subjects. Programmes need constant refreshment with new contributors.

Another vital source is social activity. This can mean no more than the man sitting next to the producer at last night's dinner. Going to places where interesting people meet can produce happy events, but beware. The talkative lady who entertains you throughout the dessert with her tale of keeping wasps in her bedroom may sound very different the next day in a studio.

16.5   PUFF PASTRY

Another popular source is P.R. handouts. Authors, playwrights, pop stars, politicians, businessmen; all have their public-relations people working over-time to cajole the media into offering a free puff. Unfortunately, too much air time is taken up with these thinly-veiled excuses to advertise the latest product. The only virtue puffing has is cheapness. Authors promoting their latest novel are usually too relieved or ashamed to demand a fee.

16.6   HEAVY OR LIGHT FARE

There is also the question of tone. You may choose to keep your programme serious throughout. Or try for lighter items. There is a place for everything. Much will depend on the programme's brief. Is it to illuminate the major news stories of the day? Or bring advice to a special group? Content is limited by the brief and also by the nature of the programme format.

Wherever the ideas come from, they have to be fashioned into radio. On a magazine you have a variety of options but they must be considered within the overall shape of the show.

16.7   A BALANCED DIET

You cannot have a programme confined to interviews. Its predictability would be no better if your choice was restricted to talks or 'straight' pieces. Even several successive miniature documentaries, featurettes or packages would be no better. 'Magazine' suggests a mixture and that has proved the most successful formula. There is nothing to stop you having two interviews, one after another. But if the first is done by your presenter, the second could be by a reporter. If your presenter is male, the second item could be done by a woman. If the first interviewee is female, the second could be male.

You may think this is putting the cart before the horse, but balance in a magazine is not just a question of content; it also concerns the colour of sound and the dynamic of the programme.

The dynamic of the programme. Sounds good. But does it mean anything? It means a sense of forward movement, while at the same time giving the appropriate weight to items. It means a balance within the programme that satisfies the listener. Dynamic also relates to the duration of the programme which, in turn, dictates the duration of the items within it.

How many items should a thirty-minute magazine have? We have already spent thirty seconds arriving at the first cue to the first item. If we assume an average cue of thirty seconds, and an average item length of three minutes, this brings us to twenty-eight minutes thirty seconds after eight items. The presenter may have something to say and there may well be playout music at the end. Let's assume this brings us to twenty-nine minutes dead. Not far off the required length of time.

In fact, thirty-minute programmes in the BBC do not often go beyond twenty-eight minutes thirty seconds because of the need for continuity announcers to have their say and allow a breathing space before the next programme. In commercial radio there are advertisements to consider.

Average durations are just that: average. If every cue and every item are the same length, the programme will sound too predictable. In fact straight pieces (talks) are rarely as long as three minutes. There is no hard and fast rule. I have heard dozens of talks which ran for four or five minutes and had me wanting more. But, on the whole, the single voice is best in small doses in a magazine programme. Interviews may be worth more than three minutes. Over time you will develop a sense of 'Just So', a feel for the right length of an item.

Your decisions about lengths of individual items are yours. But the schedule has the last word. Every programme must fit within its pre-ordained box. Any overrun and you crash the next programme or lose the advertisements and, perhaps, the clients who paid for them.

16.8 ENTREMETS

Like mortar between the bricks of a wall, presentation holds together the disparate elements of a magazine. A fascinating collection of items can be reduced to rubble by boring presentation whereas a ho-hum programme can be rescued by a brilliant presenter.

Presenters are as varied as the types of programmes on which they work. They may be the sort of people who present live current-affairs magazines, journalists with a gift for gab radio. Or they may be broadcasters who acquire sufficient specialist knowledge to carve a niche for themselves.

One of the fundamental difficulties for a producer is learning how to cope with different presenters. It's always hard to judge how far a presenter needs help. A degree of professional prickliness will meet the producer who encroaches too far on what the presenter considers his prerogatives.

In the BBC World Service, presenters are expected to write their own scripts, do a certain number of interviews, appear before the mic and help out with publicity trails. They may have to travel with the programme or leave the studio for an individual item. They are generally spoiled by the production staff.

Presenters of specialist programmes pride themselves on their knowledge. They may or may not have been specialists before they started on the programme but, in any case, as producers come and producers go, it doesn't take long for a presenter to be more knowledgeable about the programme and the necessary contacts than anyone else in the office. Young producers run the danger of being reduced to admiring slaves, at the presenter's beck and call.

Another point of pride for specialist current-affairs presenters lies in devising their own line of questioning for interviews and providing a script that requires no correction. It takes consummate skill for a producer to suggest another line of interrogation or run a blue pencil through a script.

Another skill of presenters of live programmes is coolness under fire. When the telephone line goes down, and the despatch from our correspondent in Venezuela with it, they glide smoothly on to the next item, trusting that the frantic figure of the producer in the cubicle will adjust the rest of the programme to fit. The presenter is also expected to do last-minute live interviews, chatting to the interviewee during the few minutes playing time of a pre-recorded interview.

Keeping to time means also being able to cut script on demand or, much more difficult, fill to time at no notice.

16.9 DESSERT

The BBC World Service presenter Colin Hamilton was presenting an edition of the World Service magazine 'Outlook'. His producer informed him that he would have to fill a little. Most human beings are incapable of speaking about themselves for a minute at a stretch. Five minutes of busking about a lost recipe for banana pie is stretching things to breaking point. But that is what Colin did. It produced a flood of helpful letters suggesting what the recipe might have been.

17 SCRIPTING FOR MAGAZINES

AT MORLEY COLLEGE, students are invited to create a magazine programme at the end of their first term. They choose their items from a pre-recorded pool of their own interviews and talks. The same items tend to be chosen by each team yet no magazine programme sounds like any other. The difference lies in the scripting and presentation.

In a magazine programme the short pieces of script which bind the items together are called cues. The scripted parts of a programme or package on one subject are known as links. Links and cues are usually written by the person who will present the programme.

As we've seen, there are many kinds of magazine and each will require its own style of presentation. The programme must have a consistency of 'feel'. Presentation is the unifying factor, the tone-setter. There is no point in going against all the expectations of your listener just for the sake of it. Do not write up or down. You are not trying to prove how clever you are nor how stupid the listener is. The basic assumption of the broadcaster is that the listener is ignorant - but intelligent. Ignorant doesn't mean stupid; only lacking the information you are about to impart. So do not patronise.

The magazine script consists of various elements...

17.1 THE INTRODUCTION
What do you do when you enter a strange house for the first time? You say who you are. That's what you must do when you bring your programme into some-body else's life. Even a serious programme needn't be unfriendly. Of course, you may prefer to be introduced, in which case a continuity announcer will give the names of you and your programme. Then your first words will be a greeting to the listener.

17.2 THE MENU
We've already given examples of the menu. These vary from the succinct and informative to the jokey and teasing. The British can't pass by a good pun. (You may have deduced that Andy and I are British). Be discreet in their use. There are times when you can forgo a menu completely and move directly to your first item. Why not? If yours is the only specialist programme of its kind, listeners are unlikely to switch off for lack of a list of items. The shorter the programme the less need for a menu. For long magazines, confine your menu to a selection of items which you think will attract the listener. A complete list of fourteen items stretches patience and memory. While the menu may lure the listener on, it also removes an element of surprise.

17.3   CUES

At the end of the menu there is usually a brief pause, followed by the cliché of clichés 'But first...'. Of course it's first. It's clearly not last, or even second. It's a rare magazine-presenter who can resist those two words. In fact, a brief pause before introducing the new subject is sufficient, as newreaders have known for ever.

'The Soviet Union occupies a sixth of the world's surface. Some of its fifteen republics want to break away from the Union. Boris Yeltsin, President of the Russian Republic, by far the largest of the fifteen, supports independence. But he's also hinting that republics adjacent to Russia may be invited to make certain border-adjustments in Russia's favour. I asked Bridget Kendall, the BBC correspondent in Moscow, for the basis of Russia's claims on its neighbours.'

The standard current-affairs cue. Informative, direct, with a touch of irony in the phrase 'may be invited to make certain border-adjustments...'. Sentences build on each other. The 'union' in the second sentence echoes the same word in the first. 'Republics' is also repeated. Russia occurs several times. There's no harm in creative oral repetition. Most of the ideas will be repeated in a different form in the interview, in any case.

Notice how the first question is incorporated in the cue itself. The next voice you expect to hear is Ms. Kendall's. This technique is a useful convention. Were the question left in, you would hear the presenter's voice either recorded in a different studio or at a different distance from the mic. In either case the juxtaposition of presenter to presenter would jar. Occasionally, if the questioner's voice is different from the presenter's, the lead question is left in.

The next cue begins...

'The BBC's Bridget Kendall in Moscow on Boris Yeltsin's territorial warning.'

This is known as a back-announcement. It serves two purposes; to identify who has been speaking, for the listener who needs reminding and for the listener who switched on late and missed the opening cue. The listener may only have half an ear on the cue-in to the piece but becomes interested as it goes along. The back-announcement will satisfy newly aroused curiosity about the participants. If it's a package lasting several minutes then memory may fail.

In radio there's an old adage 'Tell them it's coming, tell them it's here, tell them what they've just heard.'

Incidentally, if you think back-announcements are a waste of time, try listening to a long magazine programme without them.

The second cue continues...

'In New York today a subway train ran into a pillar underground. In the darkness, five people died and many more were injured. The driver has been arrested and charged with manslaughter after a substance was found in his cab by police. From New York, the BBC's John Smith.'

The report begins...

'In New York today a crowded subway train crashed. Investigators found that the train had jumped the rails and collided with a pillar. Police reported five people dead and many more injured...'

You're right. There's not much difference between the cue and the beginning of the report. Imagine the reporter's feelings. He has struggled to glean the facts of a story which he knows will make the morning programme. He has been awake half the night yet he is elated. Then he hears the result. The presenter has stolen his thunder. The essence of the story is contained within the first two lines of the cue.

This kind of introduction is a hangover from written journalism. In newspapers there is always a strong lead paragraph containing the essential facts. If you want more detail, read on; if not, skip it. In radio, alas, you can't 'skip it'. The sound goes on. If the report simply repeats the cue then the bored listener pours a coffee, chats to the cat or switches to another station.

'New Yorkers say their city is the most exciting in the world. It's also pretty dangerous. Muggings and robberies are a daily occurrence. Travellers are wary of entering the subway stations alone at night. At the root of much of the crime is a major social problem – drug abuse. But even hardened New Yorkers were shocked to hear of the latest drugs-related crime on the subway system. The BBC's John Smith reports from New York.'

Whatever else you may say of it, this version of the cue ushers the Smith story onto the air rather than blocking its way.

Another use for the cue is to supply information which may be necessary to comprehend the item but has been excluded by accident or design. This is particularly true when an interviewee uses initials or abbreviations for organisations unfamiliar to the listener. Then again, the name of a statesman may be used without any reference to his country. This is established in the cue.

The purpose of good presentation is to give the listener every chance of deriving the full benefit from the programme. In a way it's like a discreet detective novel with the clues placed in full view.

The presenter goes on writing cues for the magazine until the final back announcement. Then there is the 'pay-off'. How you say good-bye is as important as how you greet your listener. Identify the programme and yourself once more and offer an invitation to the next edition. You do want your listener back.

17.4 ACTION POINTS:

Before writing anything, read any research material as well as any draft cues by the producer or contributor. Above all, if possible, listen to the piece. It is astonishing how many presenters fail to do this. Unless you listen, you may kill the piece by false cueing.

- Say it before you write it.
- Do not over-write. You should know how long your cues should be.
- Check your cue against the opening of the item, if it is recorded. Does it match? Are you saying 'she' when the opening word is 'they'?
- Beware of ruining a piece by mis-cueing. You may despise the subject but it isn't your job to belittle the item.
- Do not mock or test the listener's intelligence.
- Beware of using language that does not match the programme's tone.
- Read your cues to the producer of the programme or a colleague.

A second pair of ears may prevent disasters.

- Your script needs to be professionally laid out – read the next chapter.

18 LAYING IT ON THE LINE: SCRIPT LAYOUT

WRITING a wonderful script is not enough. You've also got to make it look good. There are too many tales of optimistic freelances turning up to studio recording sessions with a half-completed handwritten scrawl on toilet paper.

18.1 WHY YOU NEED A GOOD-LOOKING SCRIPT

There are several reasons why a well laid out typed script is vital:

- You must be able to read it easily at the microphone.
- You may be relying on a Studio Manager to play-in insert tapes and discs. If s/he can't read your script, then you've got problems.
- Your producer or editor will need to check through your script – making sure that you've not libelled anyone, for example, and perhaps suggesting a cut if the piece is a little too long.

So, how do you lay out a radio script? It really doesn't matter precisely how you do it, as long as it's clear and there's plenty of space for the inevitable alterations.

18.2 SCRIPT LAYOUT EXAMPLE:

PRESENTER	..so I asked John Jones what he thought of the price of fish.
TAPE, BAND 1	Jones
	IN: I think it's terrible...
	OUT: ...and it's going to get a lot worse.
	DURATION: 38"
PRESENTER	And what about the cost of spinach? Anne Evans of the Vegetable Growers' Association.
TAPE, BAND 2	Evans
	IN: It should be coming down...
	OUT: ...certainly a very good bargain.
	DURATION: 29"
PRESENTER	Anne Evans.
DISC	Side 1 Band 2
	Boiled Beef and Carrots
	Jim Sprout and the Potatoheads
	PLAY FROM 23" IN FOR 14" THEN FADE AND HOLD UNDER:
PRESENTER	And that's it from this edition of Food Facts. Join me again at the same time next week. Until then, goodbye.

DISC   MUSIC UP.
                     ENDS CLEAN AT 2'15"

18.3 SOURCE, CONTENT, DURATION AND INSTRUCTIONS

It's a good idea to separate the information into the four categories of SOURCE, CONTENT, DURATION and INSTRUCTIONS.

Thus, in the example above, the source is always on the left, so that the operator, whether it's a separate Studio Manager or you yourself, can always see which fader to open.

The content is in the middle – the text being read, or the details of the disc. Information relating to the duration of items should appear on the right, thus leaving plenty of space down this margin for time-calculations, particularly back-timings (see under TIME).

It's helpful if specific technical instructions – when to fade a disc, or when to start the background atmosphere tape which will transport your listener to the desired location so effectively – are differentiated by being typed in capitals. This information should appear in the central part of the script.

A selection of coloured highlighter pens will help to make a well prepared script even clearer.

Thus, the overall plan is this:

SOURCE	CONTENT	DURATION
AND		AND
INSTRUCTIONS		TIME CALCULATIONS

18.4 MAGAZINE LAYOUT

Magazine script layout should be just the same as above, with a couple of modifications:

- Use a separate sheet for each item. This means that the order can be changed quickly and easily, and items dropped or added with a minimum of likely confusion.
- Put a heading at the top of each page, giving the programme title and date. In a busy production office or studio, this will avoid confusion with other programmes or other editions of the same programme.
- Make sure there's a separate 'Running Order' with a list of the items in the correct order. This separate sheet can be updated or replaced as necessary, and can also be used for overall time-calculations.

19 BY ANY OTHER NAME: DOCUMENTARIES AND FEATURES

ALL DOCUMENTARIES are features but not all features are documentaries.

There's a lot of confusion about definitions when you come to this neck of the radio woods. Unfortunately, there was no precise point in time when an honoured figure in the history of broadcasting invented a format and decided to call it a documentary. In the end the definition depends on the definer.

Think of the cinema, which pre-dated radio. Film-makers talked about 'feature films'. In another medium, a 'feature article' is found outside the news pages. It may contain an interview with a celebrity, it may analyse Brazil's ecological problems, it may offer whimsical thoughts on changing culinary customs.

The newspaper and radio feature have one thing in common; they deal with one subject. A feature on immigration, a feature on coalmining, a feature on the origins of the feature.

19.1 THE FEATURE

The feature programme has at its disposal all the resources of the medium. Some broadcasters say it is the second most difficult kind of programme to make, after radio drama. In fact, some of the earliest features were just that; re-creations of great historical events with the help of actors and musicians.

Sound effects, music, sound archives, written records, original writing, actors, real people, readers, every ingredient in the medium goes into the stew. It's not surprising that, at one time, drama and features huddled together in the same department.

19.2 THE DOCUMENTARY

Documentaries on the other hand – and here I am treading on very thin ice – documentaries must not contain imaginary elements. They do not guess what Raleigh might have said when Elizabeth I muddied his best cloak. Documentaries do not invent material: that is why they are documents. They represent actuality, whether of the 1930s or today.

The voices they contain are the voices of real people. Wherever possible, the letters they quote were written by historical characters, not script-writers.

This doesn't mean that the documentary is 'truer' than the feature. After all, a novel may tell you more about life than a text-book on anthropology or psychology. It is simply a question of definition.

All the lessons in interviewing, talks, script-writing, editing and the use of effects will come together in making a documentary. And, unlike radio drama, the documentary only requires one broadcaster and a tape-recorder.

19.3 THE AUTHORIAL VOICE

Ingmar Bergman's films are a product of his own genius. He wrote the scripts; found the money, the actors, the crew; directed, and edited his own work. Such film-making is called 'auteur' (author) production. Bergman shares credit or blame with no-one for his films.

The technical media in Britain have not worked like that. Film and television above all have been produced by team-work, the labour shared among specialists. The one opportunity for 'auteur' creation of a large work is in the documentary field of radio.

Here's how you, the loner, could set about it.

19.4 PROBLEMS

First of all you must be aware that you are going to face problems of pace and dynamics. Keeping the listener's attention for the four or five minutes' duration of a package is one thing; holding it for the fifteen, thirty or even sixty minutes of a documentary is a much tougher proposition.

So, when you propose your idea, make sure it will carry the weight. A good documentary will need editing down to make it fit. If you need to scramble to find additional material after what you hoped was the final cut, the subject is too thin.

Tone is also difficult to maintain over long periods of time. The lighter the tone, the more it will grate after the first few minutes. (This caveat does not apply to the comic genius.) Too even a tone will tend to bore after a while, whether light or serious.

19.5 PROPOSAL

Write down your idea. Explain what your programme sets out to do. Whom will you speak to? How much will it cost? How long will it take to finish? Enthusiasm is insufficient. The process of convincing others about your idea will help to clarify things for you.

Once you have reached agreement you need to plan your production schedule. Stage one is research, although much of this will have already preceded the presentation of your idea.

19.6 PREPARATION

Most documentaries depend on 'actuality', the recording of real events and people. Arrangements, we have already noted, always take longer than you think. Set about them yesterday, you haven't a moment to lose. People have a peculiar habit of going on holiday the day after you meant to ring them and didn't.

Explain fully what you intend to do with the interview. Point out that in a documentary it will not necessarily be broadcast in its entirety. If asked, disclose who else will be in the programme. If money is involved, bring it out into the open. If you have none, say so. Above all, do not make assurances you cannot fulfil.

You may have a firm idea of what you want to hear on the air but be prepared – life is not predictable. Don't be afraid to follow the trail wherever it leads. Dead ends face you but so do sudden, startling panoramas.

19.7   PEARLS

One useful technique for designing a documentary is what I call 'the string of pearls'. Find a good interviewee who knows more about the subject of your programme than you need. Record an interview, exploring all the avenues you can. Edit the interview into its more interesting parts, carefully timing the inserts and annotating the questions you are cutting out. Such information is invaluable when it comes to scripting your programme.

Next, interview your other contributors, people whose knowledge may be deeper in parts although not so wide. As new voices express ideas with greater lucidity, or offer deeper insights, use them to replace the appropriate parts of the original interview.

The original interview is the string on which you are threading the pearls.

19.8   PROOF

However you edit your material, whatever you include in your script, you must be sure in your own mind that you can justify it. Can you substantiate your evidence? Have you displayed the evidence in such a way as to justify your conclusions? Have you been fair? And honest?

19.9   PINTS AND QUARTS

Many documentary makers tend to go for overkill. They record too much and then worry about squeezing everybody into the programme. If this leads to distortion of what a contributor wished to say then it is better to leave out the contribution completely. Omission is preferable to misrepresentation.

19.10   PREJUDICE

There is also a problem about endings. Should your programme come to a firm conclusion? Is it right to editorialise? Or should you be content simply to present the evidence and allow the listener to draw a conclusion?

Unfortunately there is no way to avoid accusations of bias in a documentary. Radio is a linear medium. You cannot present evidence side by side simultaneously. One item precedes another. Somebody has to have the last word. Whom do you choose? If the first thirty seconds of a programme are decisive in persuading the listener to stay tuned, the last thirty may be decisive in shaping his view of a subject. It is preferable, in my opinion, to present sound evidence and come to a conclusion which clearly derives from it, than to avoid the issue. The chances are that those who oppose your conclusion will remain unconvinced anyway, so there is no point, only pain, in sitting on the fence.

19.11   PRACTICALITIES

Let's get back to basic methodology. Here you are at the editing machine with a heap of five-inch reels of quater-inch tape from your Uher portable machine or seven-inch reels dubbed from your cassette recorder.

Where do you begin?

First you need editing materials – chinagraph pencil, sticky tape, one-sided razor blade, editing block. Then you require a thick notebook, a pen and a stop-watch. Your first task is to annotate all your material, timing as you go.

Become as familiar as possible with the material before you begin to edit. There is no point in spending hours cutting material that will finish in the waste bin. This is the moment when you regret recording ten hours' worth of interviews for a thirty-minute programme. In film terms that is a twenty-to-one shooting ratio. Clever documentary makers can make do with four or five to one.

19.12   EDITING

When you have finished annotating and timing, you can begin to edit. (For all you need to know about the mechanics of editing, see Chapter 9.) Really clever editors decide on the order of inserts from their notes before they begin, and skip from reel to reel of raw material, building up a sequential master-tape as they go. You will develop a rhythm when doing a great deal of editing.

Editing a half-hour documentary may well take days.

You can, if you wish, create an entire documentary just by cutting pieces of tape end-to-end on one reel. But if you wish to cross-fade or hold music under the actuality or touch in your own actual sound effects then you are going to have to be subtler.

In film-making there is a way of editing called A and B roll. A similar technique may be used in radio. This involves dividing your material between two or more reels. Place all music and sound effects on one reel, for instance, and all speech on another. This enables you to fade in and out as required.

It is a good idea to dub music onto quarter-inch tape from CD or Vinyl Disc. The fewer the pieces of machinery to be played, the easier the task of assembling the programme.

Once you have rough-cut the material, you will usually find you still have too much. The next stage of editing is more difficult. Now you are rejecting material you sweated blood to get. But time is the harshest task-master. Your programme cannot run to thirty-one minutes thirty.

19.13 RATIOS

There is no hard-and-fast rule about the ratio of inserts to script in a documentary. There are documentaries with no script at all, just actuality re-assembled. In others, the script predominates.

A rough guide is two minutes of inserts for every minute of script. Let's say, nineteen minutes of tape and nine and a half of studio presentation.

19.14 OVERTURE

How to start? The old question about signature tunes raises its head. Or should you select a strong piece of actuality to grab the listener's attention before the presenter speaks? Or what about a montage? Or a sound-effect?

It is difficult to avoid predictability. Any technique you use will have been tried before but at least let it be fresh for you. Your editor may have heard it; the same will not apply to every listener. But beware of striving for novelty for its own sake. The rest of the programme must justify the opening.

19.15 ANOTHER HEAD

In an 'auteur' documentary you will have to write your own script and voice it. It is your programme. This holds certain risks.

Radio and television are regarded differently from newspapers in terms of editorial licence. The BBC, in particular, feels it must be seen as non-partisan.

Impartiality in the past meant that documentaries tended to be produced by a BBC staff member, while presentation was handled by an outsider, a free-lance contributor. Two heads, it was suggested, are better than one.

If you are presenting your own programme, be sure that you let somebody you trust check your material before it is broadcast.

Apart from spotting obvious errors of language or fact that have become invisible to you during weeks of close-up work with the material, a wise head can point out the dangers of libel.

19.16   HILLS AND VALLEYS

As with the package, the documentary script should be woven into the texture of the programme. No 'that was' or 'this is'. No current-affairs magazine programme clichés. The pattern of a documentary should be an unbroken line of curving hills and valleys, the script and inserts forming a seamless whole.

There is no 'logic' to a documentary programme, except the logic of association. Your script will echo words used by other protagonists, pick up ideas expressed in the previous insert to carry them forward to the next, give the listener a sense of progress to a conclusion.

The script serves another purpose. Some of the material in the waste bin contained valuable information. When a contributor mangles the information and takes too long expressing it, the presenter must replace the garbled prolixity with a taut link. If a contributor should mention a name, an acronym or any other term that requires it, the presenter supplies a discreet gloss.

One of the main problems of scriptwriting is identification of contributors. In a magazine programme you will back-announce an interview with John Smith. But, in a documentary in which John Smith reappears several times, simple back-announcements are tedious. You must try to incorporate the name of the speaker into the script in an unobtrusive manner.

'So much for the problem of impartiality. But John Smith's argument that no broadcaster is capable of true impartiality is echoed by Sir Stokely Pugh.' Not the most elegant of links but preferable to endless repetitions of the formula: 'John Smith. But who shares his views? Sir Stokely Pugh.'

19.17   TROUBLEMAKER

The documentary has caused more trouble in radio and television than any other form. In a world dominated by three-second sound-bites the documentary takes its time. It lifts stones. It investigates. It opines.

Dangerous practices. As radio evolves, the documentary could be one of the casualties of fragmentation and commercialisation. Certain politicians would be glad to see the back of it.

On the other hand, small, lively radio stations may in future adopt the more partisan political approach of newspapers. In which case those politicians who now clamour for the diminution of the power of large broadcasting organisations will sigh for the days when a documentary paid scrupulous attention to the objective and impartial presentation of evidence before reaching a tentative conclusion. On the other hand...

20 HOT AIR: DISCUSSIONS

THE DISCUSSION is one of the most difficult things to do well on radio. A young producer on 'Outlook' had an idea. The subject was humour. The idea was to invite three comedians to the studio and, under the guidance of the programme presenter, discuss what makes people laugh.

Having had the idea, the producer set about the task with relish, tracking down three of Britain's best comedians for the programme. The result was a disaster: one of the guests was somewhat undisciplined, the others lugubrious. Comedians take their profession seriously.

It is not enough to throw a group of interesting people together in a studio and stand back, waiting for brilliant repartee. Discussions need a lot of pre-planning. Those wonderful, spontaneous, free-wheeling talk-shows are the product of a great deal of sweat.

20.1 DEFINITION

The first question the producer must ask is whether the subject is right for this particular radio format. The discussion is not the means of disseminating pure information. Nor is it just conversation. A discussion is structured talk between knowledgeable speakers who do not often agree.

I am sure that there are instances of discussions between like-minded people, tumbling over each other to praise the same government policies. I am sure they were interesting, if a little lop-sided. But were they exhilarating? Or exciting?

Portraying differing views by differing protagonists about a subject can be done equally well by the package or documentary. But these two formats are controlled by the broadcaster and his trusty editing blade. The discussion puts more of the onus on the protagonists. There is no explanatory linking script, no sound-effects, no music to inject a change of pace; just a group of voices, arguing a case with passionate reason.

20.2 THE CHAIR

Once a subject has been agreed, the next task is to find your speakers. The most important is the chairperson or, if you prefer, 'chair'. Concentration, quick-wittedness, discipline and respectability are just some of the qualities a good chairperson needs.

Why didn't I include 'knowledge' in the list? As with interviewers, so with chairpersons. Put an expert against another expert and the loser is the listener, as the broadcasters soar into aerial regions beyond the reach of any but eagles.

What is required is a good broadcaster, perhaps a specialist in politics or economics, if that's what the programme is about, but, above all, aware of the needs of the medium and the programme, able to communicate with the producer as well as the contributors; the respected professional guide who relieves the studio guests of most of their burdens.

Once the invitation from the producer has been accepted, the chairperson may offer suggestions on contributors. The subject will be studied in detail and a broad shape for the programme agreed in terms of areas to be covered. Usually the chairperson is required to write an introduction to the programme and the contributors.

20.3   INTROS

Fashions in radio change. Introductions are tending to become more risqué, more pointed, than they were in the past. They have also tended to become longer, a display of the wit of the chairperson taking up the first two minutes of the broadcast. Other chairs seem to subscribe to the brevity-is-the-soul-of school.

20.4   THE CAST

The producer and the chairperson have contacted the contributors and discovered that politician A refuses to be in the same studio as B, while B has an aversion to X. But in the end the cast are selected. To the producer's delight he has a good range of voices, easily distinguished from one another. Two men, one tenor, the other baritone and an eminent sociologist mezzosoprano (female).

20.5   SOCIALISING

The group assembles in the producer's office half an hour before the recording. (Many discussions go out live; recording allows a certain leeway for editing, particularly the earlier minutes during which the panel are 'warming up').

It may not be advisable to offer alcohol; on the other hand... The talk is aimed at allowing the panel to get the feel of each other. Whatever you do, do not discuss the subject of the programme, except obliquely. If the arguments are rehearsed in advance, all spontaneity is lost.

20.6   INSTRUCTIONS

In the studio the chairperson faces the cubicle where the producer and studio manager listen. The chairperson is wearing headphones. He is the only person who can hear instructions from the cubicle. He begins with a little homily along these lines.

'In a moment or two we'll be taking level – seeing how your voice sounds. We may adjust the microphone's position, or yours, but once level has been taken, please stay in that position. If you move away from the microphone your voice will sound odd; and even odder if you move in closer. Please address all your remarks to me even if you're replying to a neighbour. If you turn your head away from the mic. your voice will be lost. By the way, would you mind removing your leather jacket? I'm afraid it creaks. Oh, and your bracelet. The mic. picks up every sound.'

Level is taken and then the chairperson delivers the following oration:

'Just a word about names. If you use first names from the beginning of the programme, it sounds a little too cosy, not so much a discussion, more a chat between friends. For the first few minutes, would you mind addressing each other by your usual first name and surname. Once I introduce you by your first name only, you can follow my lead. Please remember that this is a discussion. I shall try to bring everyone in and keep a fair balance. Resist the temptation to make all your points at once – confine yourself to one at a time.

'There are some main areas that we've agreed to discuss and I shall try to introduce them all. Within these areas I hope the talk will move freely between you. Don't be afraid of interrupting; but before you do, please indicate your intention by raising a finger. I will catch the eye of the person speaking and point at the next speaker. The person speaking shouldn't stop in mid-sentence but complete the sense of what is being said.

'The point of the exercise is to allow me to introduce you by name. Remember, the listener is blind and your voices will need identifying. Also, if you all speak at once it becomes confusing for the listener to a monaural transistor radio. Now, are there any questions? Good. Then, one last task before we begin; I'll read you my brief introduction. If I've got anything wrong, now is your chance to correct it.'

20.7   LIVE DISCUSSIONS

If you have the luxury of a producer in the cubicle beyond the glass, you will rest easier about timings and the dynamics of the programme. You can spend more of your time listening. The producer cannot jump in to save the situation if the contributors get in a tangle or if something needs explanation. You can. You will also be aware of how the argument is flowing.

20.8   THE PRODUCER...

...will be taking notes of the contributions. As producer, you will need to know how many times each speaker has spoken and in what order. The chair may be going round the table in the same order each time. If so, you will need to change things with a gentle remark through the talk-back. Choose your moment; even the most experienced chairpersons come unstuck if they're talking and a voice mutters in their ear. Since you're listing the contributions, you might as well mark down the timings as well. A fair distribution of air time is what you're trying to achieve. This doesn't mean equal shares to the second, but rough parity. Timing is of vital importance to your chairperson as well. By pre-arrangement you will give signals as you approach the end of the programme. Some people prefer flashing lights but this can be distracting for the contributors. The alternative is hand signals.

One minute   **Half a minute**   **Wind-up**   **Cut**

20.9   EDITING

If your programme is pre-recorded then you will have the opportunity to 'clean it up' afterwards. You may have anticipated a difficult first few minutes while the contributors warmed to their subject and so agreed with your chairperson to lengthen the recording for the purposes of editing. As with all other editing, your job is to improve the programme material while remaining fair to the spirit of the contributions. So while cutting to time you need to retain balance.

One additional point about editing. The question is whether to 'de-um' or not. 'De-umming' means taking out those tiny mistakes (fluffs), repeats, coughs and other extraneous noises that can occur in any broadcast. Some people can take the cleaning up process too far by shortening pregnant pauses and making their speakers sound pluperfect. Others believe in warts-and-all broadcasting with everything left in. Perhaps the conventional British compromise is best: retain what adds to the character of the programme, remove what is clearly undesirable.

21 MAKE MINE MUSIC

MUSIC is one of the three legs of radio. With speech and effects it makes up the sound tripod.

Music is legally cheap and illegally expensive. The use of music is hedged round with all kinds of agreements, with all kinds of organisations. You may even find that the playing of certain kinds of offensive music is forbidden by your station management.

Stations that depend on music for the majority of their output will be well aware of the do's and don'ts of the law. It tends to be makers of speech-based programming who get into hot water when they try to include 'a few notes of music'.

There's the legendary case of the young producer who went to do an item on an orchestra and thought it would be a good idea to record the conductor at work. Just a few seconds of a rehearsal with the maestro stopping the musicians in order to proffer a friendly word of advice on how to extract the best from bar thirty-nine.

The story ends in tears. After the extract was broadcast, the station was presented with a very large bill for the services of over a hundred musicians, all solid members of the union and covered by agreements. Even with amateur performers it's advisable to get a signature on a waiver before broadcasting any part of a performance.

I can vouch for the following story. We decided to record an item on tea-dancing at a famous London hotel not far from Bush House. The freelance contributor persuaded me to be her dancing partner. (A Uher portable open-reel tape recorder is rather heavy). All the arragements had been made with the hotel mnagement. We sailed forth.

We danced around the floor, pausing from time to time to question other dancers. Welcome refreshment persuaded us to retire to a nearby table. No sooner were we settled, than the leader of the small band appeared. He politely enquired whether we had recorded any music. When I replied in the affirmative, he demanded a fee somewhat in excess of that being paid to the contributor for the whole package.

The band-leader explained without malice that he and the lads were tired of being ripped off by the management and every kind of television and radio broadcaster for the sake of 'good public relations'. No compromise could be arrived at. In the end we used only those interviews recorded between dances and created atmosphere with music from a record.

Needle-time is the name given to the total amount of music that a particular station can play from disc. It has to be paid for in several different ways. Every single second of music played on the air is detailed; duration, title, name of composer, disc identification. This is to enable the copyright people to pass on to the artists an agreed share of the money broadcasters pay for the privilege of playing their music on air.

In many parts of the world, the law, civil or criminal, is unconcerned with the recording or pirating of music. Folk music tends to escape, as does non-professional performance. In parts of China, kindergarten children routinely sing for media visitors. Ceremonial occasions with military or colliery bands of all sorts also appear on the air.

Even in Britain there are limits to what can be legalised. Imagine asking each member of a Wembley Cup Final crowd for written permission to broadcast 'Abide With Me'.

21.1 MUSIC PRODUCTION VALUES

There are those, we have already noted, who detest music on speech radio. It's not just a question of 'old-fashioned' sig. tunes. Any music.

The rule must be – play music where music is appropriate. Do not squeeze music into every available crack. A well-chosen, timely excerpt may lift a good piece of radio to the level of the sublime. Inappropriate music will make your listener wince or snigger.

On the other hand do not reduce music to the punctuation mark. If you do feel it should be used, give it time to breathe. An item on Schubert needs more than ten seconds of the overture to 'Rosamunde' before rushing on to the next cue.

The use of music on speech radio is partly a question of 'feel', partly a question of technique. There are certain ground rules.

Music can set a mood. A radio play or feature programme will often begin with some evocative musical phrases designed to attune the listener's emotions. Just as the rattle of biscuits in a dog's bowl sets the animal's salivary glands working, so a lively piece of intro music can raise the expectations of an audience to a quiz or comedy programme.

Music may act as a signpost. In magazine programmes the musical 'sting', a brief burst of music, usually derived from the signature tune, will mark the end of an item, indicating a change of subject and pace. The obvious danger is over-using the sting or using it in a tasteless manner. An item on the loss of lives in an accident shouldn't be followed by a cheerful burst of jingle.

Music can be used to introduce related items in a more exciting way. For example, after a back-announcement, followed by a heart-beat's pause, you play a montage of different kinds of music, lasting a few seconds each. Fade under your cue which asks what those melodies have in common. Answer: copyright. A difficult item to sell on the basis of words alone has intrigued the listener by use of an attractive, musical teaser.

Music is a useful buffer. Playout music at the end of a programme is a device to soak up the spare seconds before the next announcement. To work for the listener it needs to relate to the preceding item.

An edition of 'Outlook' ended with an item on photographic developing and printing. Cheerful ladies talked about the problem of locating the owners of photographs who had failed to fill in their correct name and address on the package. The instrumental music came up below the last words of the item, the programme presenter paid off and the music swelled to a close. We puzzled over the choice. Then somebody recognised the tune. It was 'Some Day My Prince Will Come'.

You will notice that the producer used an instrumental version of the song. It may be tempting to mix vocal music with a voice-over presentation. Unless you are very skilful, they will detract from each other's comprehensibility. Do not mingle voices. Words should float on waves of instrumental music.

Cadences should be honoured. It cannot be repeated too often that music should be faded on a cadence rather than in the middle of a bar. The listener's ear has been so well trained to expect fades at the 'right' place that you risk a loss of confidence in your programme if you fade outside the mark.

That music to close. How on earth did we know it would end on time? Simple. Pre-fading.

Suppose your programme is to end at 21:00. The band on the record runs three minutes. Start the disc running at 20:57 with the fader closed. As the minutes and seconds flicker by, your music is there, ready to fade up and play out to time. 'No worries', as Andy would say.

Modern record-players are even cleverer. They will play forwards and backwards, timing accurately in either direction. If you know your presenter will leave you thirty seconds at the end of the show, then find the conclusion of the music, run back a minute and start the machine sixty seconds before the end of the programme, fader at the ready to bring up closing music as required. Naturally, tape machines and CD players are just as versatile. The simple arithmetic of pre-fading still holds good.

Commercial recorded music may not meet your requirements. The BBC has a successful electronic workshop for the creation of synthesised music by talented composers. Original bespoke music can give a series of programmes a mark of great distinction.

21.2 DISC JOCKEYING

The art of the D.J. lies outside the province of this course. But one or two trade secrets: how on earth does the D.J. know how long to talk over the instrumental introduction before the vocal starts? Simple: the duration is on his script. So he doesn't have to memorise the openings of the top hundred.

Nowadays, computers have come into their own and almost anybody can perform the basic tasks of the D.J.

In the primitive days of rock radio the record presenter had to have good coordination to cope with microphone faders, setting up vinyl discs, holding scripts or reader's letters and worrying about tape cartridges.

Today, a computer controls; the order of play of the C.D.s, the digital bank of commercials, and the overall timing of the programme. A print-out informs the presenter of the position each song reached on the hit parade and when.

If you want to be a D.J. the easy way, buy yourself a software programme. Combine that with a touch screen and you can play tennis with your free hand.

22 DIGITS

The sound and vision world is rapidly changing from the old-fashioned analogue technology to the new digital systems. So what's the big deal?

The new technologies became possible because engineers began to apply the techniques of computers to audio (and then video) equipment. Computers can now do just about anything with sound, provided that it can be translated into the binary digits ('bits') that the machine needs.

22.1 DIGITAL ADVANTAGES:

- No distortion;
- No hiss or other interference;
- More robust signals - less chance of corruption;
- Copies are identical to the original - there's no degradation in copying;
- Easier and cheaper to transfer signals from place to place;
- New methods of editing and mixing;
- Systems becoming ever cheaper.

Compared with these advantages, older analogue systems can only really compete on the basis of familiarity and a hands-on, tactile element which appeals to some people. And also, there's a lot of good second-hand analogue equipment available as studios upgrade.

There is one technical disadvantage: if an analogue system goes wrong, it often gives warning and can be nursed along with a small loss of quality. If a digital system crashes, it's a complete failure and you can't do anything until the nice engineer comes.

22.2 HOW DOES IT WORK?

Instead of conventional systems, which attempt to provide an electrical mimic of the varying sound waves, digital systems carve up the sound into tiny slices which are then stored or transmitted or manipulated purely as numbers. Further, they are reduced to binary numbers - either 0s or 1s. It's like a set of light switches: they are either on or off. There's no question of "was it 58 or was it 59?".

The tiny slices are taken as many as 44,100 times a second. This is called the sampling rate. 44,100 is the rate for compact discs - other systems can use other rates. If you want to get technical, you need a sampling rate 2.2 times the frequency of the highest sound you want to reproduce. So 44,100 will give you a top frequency of about 20 kilohertz - the highest note you can hear when you're young and haven't been to too many discos or worked in a sheet-metal factory.

Analogue distortion

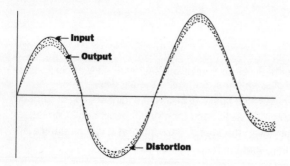

Digital sampling of an analogue signal

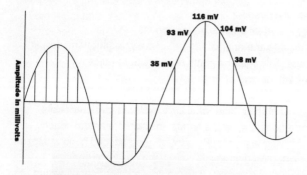

Digital distortion doesn't damage

Amplitudes are turned into ditigal numbers –
0's or 1's – which appear as pulses

Even if they get a little fuzzy . . .

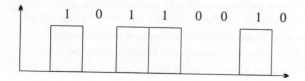

. . . they can be reconstructed exactly

22.3 PRACTICAL SYSTEMS

Digital systems have an impact on all areas of radio.

a Recording

Portable digital recorders are becoming as common as the ubiquitous professional cassette machines. And they're not much more expensive. DAT is the commonest form, but there are several other systems. As with previous electronic revolutions, it's anybody's guess which system will triumph. It's most likely that the final result will be an all-solid-state gadget with no moving parts.

And of course compact discs have been providing digital technology and quality in ordinary homes for more than a decade.

b Editing and mixing

This is an area which has seen the development of a huge array of different systems, at widely varying prices. All of them use a computer, and most of them are mouse or touch-screen driven. Some machines are much more suitable for the music recording industry. Others, like the system pictured below, are aimed at radio production and have been developed in collaboration with programme-makers.

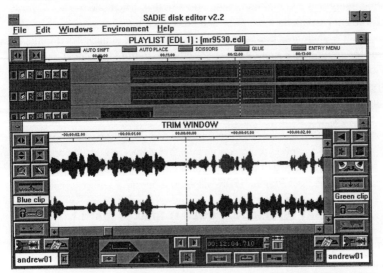

A typical computer screen from the SADiE digital editing system.

Compared with analogue systems, the digital system above puts total control in the hands of the operator. You can feed in your carefully-gathered actuality, interviews, compact discs, and suddenly you're dealing with just one technology. You have your very own complete studio on screen wherever you have a computer.

And when you're not actually making radio, you can write a book on the same computer - after all, it's still a word-processor.

A disadvantage of some systems is that material has to be 'uploaded' into the machine in real time before you can work on it. This means that fifteen minutes of interviews etc will take fifteen minutes to load. And fifteen minutes to download when you've finished working on it.

So the systems are better suited to drama, documentaries, features, advertisements etc where the time factor is less crucial and you haven't the looming deadlines which news lives by.

c Transmission

This is still in the future for most radio listeners. There's a system called Digital Audio Broadcasting (DAB) which promises CD quality, and more channels.

d Links

One area where digital systems are having an increasing impact is the point-to-point links that radio broadcasters need for gathering and disseminating their sound. Whereas the reporter of old would file his or her story down a noisy, distorted telephone line that had taken hours to dial, the modern correspondent just opens a suitcase and powers up a digital satellite telephone. It's a hundred per cent reliable, and so's the quality. The trouble is, it no longer sounds as if s/he's anywhere other than the studio next door!

Another development is the ISDN (Integrated Services Digital Network) system. In essence, this allows the transmission of digital signals down an ordinary telephone line. All you need is an encoder/decoder unit each end - and these are small and simple. You then decide what quality of line you need. Speech? Music? Stereo? You pays your money and you takes your choice. There's no longer any need to book a special line weeks in advance and to liaise with the bureaucracy of telecommunications companies. So next time you hear a concert from Prague, ISDN will almost certainly be responsible.

22.4 BUT WHAT DIFFERENCE DOES IT REALLY MAKE?

It sounds better, it can be easier to use, it's getting cheaper. But it can also lead the unwary into wasting large amounts of time. Just because every variable can be varied in infinitesimal steps means that there's a terrible temptation to worry at your material in the vain hope of improving it still further. Perfection recedes from your outstretched grasp.

At the moment, we can still compare analogue with digital, and leave it up to you to make the choice. But there is no doubt whatsoever that the industry is heading in the digital direction for two simple reasons: money and money.

The first set of savings comes from having one person making an entire radio programme.

And the second set of savings comes from the relative cheapness of replacing an entire radio studio and cubicle complex with a home-based computer and ancillary equipment.

But whether you're using Edison's original wax cylinders or the amazing Futuroscope, a lousy interview in a poor acoustic is still a lousy interview in a poor acoustic. And a bad edit is still a bad edit.

And if you can't hear the difference, then it doesn't matter whether you use a rusty razor blade or the latest digital zapper.

It's all about using your ears.

23 SO WHAT'S NEWS

News is not necessarily new - at least, not in the sense of uniquely new. Anglo-Saxon journalists would disagree. News must be unique, they say, not simply the retelling of familiar stories.

To people in Britain or the United States news is that familiar litany of wars, disasters, scandals, political punch-ups and the occasional triumph when an athlete wins a gold medal or a couch potato wins a lottery. Of course, nothing is really new. Wars, disasters and scandals have been going on since history began. (Think of Suetonius and his account of the goings-on of the Roman Emperors. Pretentious? Moi?) What people mean about 'new' is that the public have forgotten the last story on the subject. (Journalists have to rely on the forgetfulness of their listeners.)

But there's another kind of news. Good news. The people who are most familiar with this kind of news are listeners to radio in totalitarian states. News is regarded as so important to the peace and prosperity of the country that the state keeps a firm control on everything that's broadcast. The people must not for a moment doubt that everything in the totalitarian garden is rosy. And isn't the news good! Record harvests, record exports, meeting production targets, happy birthday Mr. President.

UNESCO (the United Nations Educational, Scientific and Cultural Organisation) once tried to come up with a master plan for changing the world's (well, the Western world's) view on news and current affairs. It was called the New World Information Order. UNESCO had noticed that four or five major Western news agencies dominated the sourcing of news; Western companies controlled the technology of information flows; Western views on what constitutes news dominated the agenda. So Africa was a fertile field for wars, disasters and scandals. But there was nothing about the successes because record harvests, even when true, are boring.

News, says the Third World, creates disaffection and rebellion in unstable, new societies.

So what can news be? How does it really work?

23.1 THE CIRCLES OF YOUR MIND

Ask yourself what interests you most. The answer, if an honest one, will be - 'Me'. Unless you are a famous footballer, a rock star or a great D.J. you are unlikely to feature on a radio news broadcast. What comes after you? Your friends and family. But they will inform you and others who are interested in their news via their own bush telegraph. Taking the concentric circles around you a little further we find - your block of flats or your street. When the local shopkeeper gets mugged and robbed, that is news, anywhere and in any society. But it is usually only of local interest. For you the story has the `wow' factor; for people on the other side of town the `really?' factor and for people fifty miles away the `yawn' factor.

Who does the story interest? The people it affects. So national stories on the whole interest the whole of society, either because they concern national totems (Princess Diana, Michael Jackson) or minorities whose fate is linked with everyone else's (riots in inner cities, tax increases for 'fat cats') or everybody (a typhoon on the way, a national railway strike).

So you can be involved in news at many levels. Most people will begin in hospital radio, with bulletins concerning patients and doctors or in local radio where the attack on the local shopkeeper, and the new pedestrian crossing, will grip your audience.

If there is dispute about what constitutes news and news priorities, there are certain basic buzz words that have real meaning for all journalists except those who have sold out to public relations.

23.2 TRUTH

This is the trickiest of all. Remember Pilate's question, "What is truth?". Truth is relative. Relative to the beholder. Of course some beholders behold better than others. Trained journalists and police officers are trained (!) to be more observant and detached than John Q. Citizen. Identity parades are notoriously unreliable things. Even words recorded on a tape recorder may be misheard or misinterpreted. Nevertheless, all good journalists aspire to get as close to the truth as possible. Journalistic truth is a stew with many ingredients.

23.3 ACCURACY

"Michael Kaye (75) . . . " Now when I read that I know that either the reporter or the typographer is being inaccurate. It should read "Michael Kaye (57) . . . "

Journalists are obsessed by little accuracies or 'facts'. Of course getting my age, weight, marital status and baldness accurately reported is no excuse for then making up stories about my relationship with Andy Popperwell. (Even if true, I may still sue you for libel).

One of the first journalistic tests you will be asked to take will offer you three or four agency versions of a simple story regarding the disappearance of a light aircraft. One report will say that the plane took off at 10.40 a.m.; the next will offer 10.34 a.m.; the third 10.42 a.m.; the last 10.34 a.m. You will be asked to write a definitive version of the story for broadcast. Most schools of journalism will insist on two sources of fact before publication. So does that mean 10.34 is right? If there were only two versions of the story and they both agreed on the time, that would be sufficient corroboration. But the multitude of times on offer suggests that 'sometime after ten thirty this morning' is your most accurate version.

23.4   OBJECTIVITY

You can be accurate without being 'objective'. By selecting your facts you may delude your listener into believing a biased picture of your subject. "Michael Kaye (aged 57), the balding, weak-kneed, flatulent, halitotic has-been" is very accurate but fails to mention my abilities as a cricketer. And the story is about a cricket match. Unfortunately the listener finds me distasteful before getting to the bit about my nine wickets for two runs. More importantly, a foreign correspondent needs all his powers of objectivity to keep his head when confronted by a war or natural disaster. Too often emotion clouds the reporting. One of the best ways of ensuring objectivity is to avoid the adjective in apposition. In other words, do not say 'the excellent Chancellor of the Exchequer'. There are many listeners who would not share your adjective. Nor will 'the tight-fisted old fart' improve matters.

23.5   BALANCE

This is one of the BBC's pets, a.k.a. 'on-the-one-hand-on-the-other-hand.' If, as the BBC once was, you are the sole source of news and current affairs, locally or nationally, then any hint of fear or favour towards anyone is regarded as a heinous crime. The BBC does not comment. It allows 'real' people to do that (including politicians!). Once upon a time a BBC Director General insisted that balance should exist within every programme. In other words, if Mr. X is interviewed, his arch-enemy, Ms.Y, must be as well. If you adhered strictly to this principle, nothing need ever be broadcast again.

REPORTER: "Hello, Ms.Y. We have an interview with Mr. X, slagging you off. In the nicest possible way. Would you like to respond?"
(Significant pause while the reporter nods, biting his lip.)
EDITOR: "Well, when is she doing the interview?"
REPORTER: "She refused. Said Mr. Y was lower than a snake's belly."
EDITOR: "Then we can't run X's interview until she agrees."

Get the picture? On the whole, editors tend to balance across time. Mr. X in today's programme; somebody speaking on behalf of Ms. Y's position ,or even a relenting Ms. Y herself, later. You must also be able to say - in the interest of balance - 'We offered Ms. Y the chance to respond but she declined.'

23.6   IMPARTIALITY

Balance is intimately connected with 'impartiality'. You may broadcast all points of view (i.e. Mr. X and Ms. Y) but in the way you write your links, ask your questions, order the responses, edit the answers, choose your 'sound-bites', be partial to one side or the other. One of the defences of political broadcasting is to say that both sides of the argument have complained of bias. Predictably both sides (or more - it is wrong to assume that every argument has only two sides) will complain of bias. This does not prove that bias does not exist. In radio bias can be suggested by the ironic tone of the human voice.

The categories I have laid out above are, of course, things to aim at, a counsel of perfection. The problems they pose are enormous. If we are not careful they can lead to a kind of inertia. I remember a colleague making a documentary and being unable to conclude it. In the final analysis, you are allowed to arrive at a conclusion. Reporters are expected to offer a view. But it must be a view that is clearly derived from the facts as presented. And those facts must be pertinent and complete. If you believe, on the basis of the best evidence, that war crimes have been committed, say so.

23.7 ONE RULE FOR THE RICH . . .

. . . and one for the poor. Too often reporters and correspondents in the West will take great care to follow the rules of news at home, aware of the sanctions possible under contempt of court and libel. Send them abroad, however, and their sense of responsibility deserts them. "Hell, I'm only in Ruritania for a week and I certainly never want to return. So I'll interview the terrorist leader and ignore the boring government propaganda. Makes a sexier story. Not objective, impartial, accurate? So sue me."

23.8 WE ARE ALL HUMAN

Reporters will sometimes allow their emotions to overcome them - listen to the recording of the commentary on the destruction of the R101 airship. The speaker finally breaks down.

Righteous indignation at outrageous, inhuman behaviour is understandable. Maybe one day we will have campaigning radio stations as we have campaigning newspapers. Perhaps the multiplication of media will eventually liberate radio from its corsets. Whatever new liberalisation sweeps through the world of radio in coming years, the basic principles will always remain as a yardstick. Striving to achieve perfection is preferable in the First, Third or Umpteenth World to engaging in flagrant lies to the order of a minister of information.

Here endeth the first lesson.

Having skipped lightly through the abstracts, let's get down to cases. What to do and who does it.

23.9 THE REPORTER

News gathering is an inverted triangle. The whole structure stands (or falls) on one human being who sits in the court-room, doorsteps the politician or ducks the shells; the reporter. The reporter may be an anonymous hack toiling for an international agency. S/he could be in Macclesfield or Malaysia. Often s/he is working for several employers, reworking material to suit several markets.

Ironically the same reporter may supply two different agencies with the same story. (So much for two sources!) This kind of reporter usually supplies news copy. This may be phoned in to a tape recorder, faxed or e-mailed. But, now that the agencies are getting into the radio business for themselves, voice pieces, actuality and interviews may be required.

Reporters for national or big regional radio stations usually sit in a room known as 'the pool'. There they wait for the luck of the draw. They may have to travel to Macclesfield. Or visit a trades union leader in South London. They may have to supply any of the types of coverage that agency hacks supply. If they do 'straights' (written and voiced pieces giving the story and some analysis) they are identified. News copy for newscasts is anonymous. National reporters in the BBC today are expected to be able to work in both radio and television - bimedialism is the order of the day. As Hi-8 cameras become the norm, all reporters will probably have to double. Unless . . .

. . . they are working for local radio. As yet, local television is an infant. Your Hi-8 is only there for you to cover that BIG story that might reach national television news. Otherwise you do all the general reporting jobs. Even sports. And pop. And religion. You will also sub-edit agency news; cut other people's copy or tapes; write your own bulletin (or 'bully') and present the whole shooting match. But that's local radio for you!

Specialist reporters are a new category in radio. Once upon a time there were reporters, who handled the dross, and correspondents who specialised in covering areas such as arts, science, foreign news and parliament. Correspondents have been pricing themselves out of the market for years. Overseas they cost five times more than the equivalent domestic correspondent. They may have a bureau or at least an office or an apartment or all three. The old-style correspondent expected to send ruminative pieces once in a way, full of exquisite English, wise saws and modern instances. He always sent 'straights' unless he interviewed a Head of State. Other interviews were beneath him. If a programme was to be done about his 'patch', he awaited the arrival of a producer to do his bidding and put the programme together.

This is changing. Correspondents there still are but each time one retires or is otherwise cannibalised, new entrants are taken on with a wider range of skills and a lower salary. There are more and more specialist reporters, doing what a correspondent used to but rather closer to the earth. There is no doubt that we have gained a lot from multi-skilling. The English language has suffered a little in the process.

23.10 SUB-EDITORS

So much for the workers at the pit face. Above ground there are literally thousands of journalists who depend for their existence on the pit workers. The lowliest form of parasitic journalistic life is the sub-editor. Not that s/he is unimportant. The sub-editor is the one who needs to know about two or more sources; requires to check spellings, grammar, style books (every newsroom and newspaper has its own book of 'dos' and 'don'ts') and the taste of the editor. The sub-editor rips the 'tape' (not the quarter-inch variety but the stuff spewing out of telex machines or computers) and in local radio reads it. S/he may receive reports from reporters over the phone for recording and editing. Whatever s/he does, s/he works to . . .

23.11 EDITORS

. . . who are older, tougher and with a wider knowledge of real ale. They may be hierarchied into 'senior' and 'duty' strata but they are the custodians of the content, style and standards of the news on their station. They have their little foibles and a million anecdotes provoked by real ale purchased by doting, toadying subs. They have seen every story come round at least four times and parade a tough cynicism that suggests dusty safari boots, Smith & Wessons and sultry ladies. In fact, they began life on the Billericay Bugle and have been with Capital Radio since it started. They do know about radio news and, beneath the cynical veneer, care about their charges, which include the sub-editors. They worry about the 'naming of parts'. When is a terrorist a freedom fighter, et cetera, et cetera? They can usually do any job better than you. Even if they never have to. Editors generally work a daytime shift. Every day. They are the news memory of the station. Subs come and go. Editors are forever.

So much for the dramatis personae . . . What about the modus operandi?

23.12 THE JOB

Imagine. The editor is reading a P.R. handout about a meeting of the Pickled Mice Society. Lois Lane, told her fate, groans inwardly but smiles outwardly. She is told her deadline. Because the nearest news bulletin is only ten minutes after the end of the meeting, she will have to write her thirty seconds and phone it in from the town hall. She knows a clerical officer whose phone he will be able to set up. Before she sets out she rings the town-hall to try and contact the President of the society in advance for a good quote. The thirty-seconder will be a nice 'tail' piece for the end of the bully (which is only three minutes). She will be able to get an interview into the daily news magazine at six p.m.

23.13 THE ONCE AND FUTURE NEWS

News is expensive. On a small commercial station there may only be a two minute bulletin on the hour. It is very tempting to forego a newsroom completely in favour of the inexpensive option of 'buying in' news from an agency. The trouble with that is that local news is ignored and the station sounds the same as every other station. News and music are the basic ingredients of most local commercial stations. As competition mounts and profit margins narrow, so the world's radio newsrooms are under increasing threat. In any case, with the development of the Internet and other information sources, the individual will be likely to want to seek and find his own news agenda. This will be a gain in depth and a loss in breadth.

22 THOSE WHO CAN'T, PRODUCE

IF you can't DJ, read the news, do interviews, report from a war zone, you can always produce.

A lot of the terminology in radio, television and film is borrowed from the theatre, the senior performing art. But some of the definitions tend to vary, depending on which side of the Atlantic invented them. For example a theatrical director in the States may be a producer in Britain. In the film and television industries producers handle the money. Directors do the beautiful things.

22.1 ORIGINS

In the old-style BBC, producers were the ideas men, often portrayed as pipe-smoking intellectuals. As the world of radio grows and the relative share of the BBC shrinks, producers, pure and simple, are becoming rarer birds.

In local and regional radio, in the World Service and elsewhere, the several skills of presentation, production and studio management are rolled into one individual, the 'broadcaster'. So where did the producer come from?

The man who presided over the first broadcasting company in Britain had a sense of mission. Lord Reith (as he became) believed radio would be a great instrument for the education of the people.

Others shared his view of the importance of the medium but not his definition of education.

During the General Strike of the 1920s the government tried to enlist the BBC's help as a part of its propaganda campaign against the strikers. The politicians failed but the war of attrition by successive administrations to erode the BBC's limited independence has continued to this day.

This pressure on radio by those who wished to mould public opinion to suit themselves assured the place of a breed of broadcaster who never appeared on air but who brought together all the elements of a broadcast; making sure, above all, that it met exacting criteria of fairness, objectivity and balance.

These 'producers' shared Reith's sense of purpose. Their quality was very high because the BBC, as a monopoly, could afford to set the highest standards. Soon the job of producer became a symbol of excellence and joined the ranks of the respectable professions.

22.2 TASKS

Today, although the writing may be on the wall for the professional designation of 'producer', the tasks of production remain, no matter how many computers take the place of people.

Producers are people who know people. They have contacts. Their contacts may be celebrated, worthy or merely interesting but producers are expected to be able to persuade others (and particularly the media-shy) to mutter into a microphone.

Contacts are simply one part of what a good producer needs. Like any journalist or intelligent radio-listener, the producer has to have a broad range of interests, knowledge and, above all, curiosity.

There are producers who do not have ideas themselves but respond creatively to other people's ideas. The producer of a quiz-show may well be developing somebody else's brain-child. Or responding to the news that a professional freelance may be about to visit a difficult or dangerous part of the world. Would the producer like something?

Ideas are not in short supply. Other things are, such as time and money. More and more, production is a question of eking out scarce resources; the producer is expected to possess accountancy skills which are more than just rudimentary.

Once an idea has been dreamed up and costed, the producer has to argue it through the system. After all, there are other producers (and freelances) who are making their offers and any one programme must fit into the overall scheme of things, the schedule.

Schedule? Programmes? What are these things? In many modern radio-stations there are no programmes as such and scheduling is a question of three or four presenter shifts interacting with a software programme of music, news and commercial breaks.

If your station is going to sound different from the others, then production decisions still have to be made. Choosing this D.J. rather than that. Inviting that live guest rather than this. Decisions limited by time and money.

22.3   TIME ZONES

Production falls into three time zones: pre-production, production and post-production.

22.4   PRE-PRODUCTION

Pre-production encompasses all the early processes that precede the actual making of the programme. The germ of any broadcast is, after all, a gleam in a broadcaster's eye. 'Why don't we do a programme about...?'

An idea. Selling the idea. Then winning a fair share of resources to bring the idea to the air. That's just the hors d'oeuvre.

Who will present your programme? In luxury radio the producer is still not heard. He will usually hire somebody else to be his mouthpiece; someone with the skills of reportage, interviewing, script-writing and presentation that are all too scarce in broadcasting.

The presenter will need to have the programme explained. Hours of discussion will be followed by perhaps days or weeks of research in archives, libraries or conversations.

Once the reporter/presenter has been found and briefed, the search is on for contributors. These may be professionals or so-called 'real people'. Politicians, somewhat surprisingly, come under the latter heading.

Professionals means broadcasters, actors, academics; people who rely on the medium for at least part of their income. Usually 'real people' are speaking ex officio - in other words, just doing their job - which means you don't have to pay them.

Politicians are only mercenary in certain circumstances. The 'BBC Guide for Producers' suggests that no payment is necessary if a politician is speaking on a matter relating to his or her representative function.

The BBC World Service, as is often the case, is the exception to the rule. Since in broadcasting to 'the whole world minus Britain' the Member of Parliament is broadcasting to 'the whole of humanity minus his constituents', payment may be in order.

What is certain is that leaders of British political parties do not accept payment in any circumstances.

Finding people is not simply a question of handing a list of names to an assistant. Contributors, particularly those with an inflated view of themselves or a proper disrespect for the media, often need cajoling. After all, the kind of money they are going to earn from a one-off contribution to your documentary is hardly likely to turn their heads.

They will want to know what the programme is about; what their part is to be in it; how much editing will be done; who else is being invited. It is astonishing how many deals have to be struck in the course of setting up a radio programme.

One well-known politician would agree to answer vexed questions in exchange for extra minutes of air-time. Another senior M.P.'s secretary always opened negotiations with the crisp question, 'Is there any money in it?' (Her Lord and Master charged twice the going rate on the grounds that he was twice the entertainment value.)

Once agreement has been reached, there is the question of logistics. When and where will any non-studio interviews take place? Travel, hotel bookings, food are some of the practical things that have to be considered. Studios have to be booked.

22.5 PRODUCTION

Unless you are working on an outside broadcast, production usually means working in a studio. In large broadcasting organisations there are production studios, where programmes are pre-recorded; and transmission studios where programmes are broadcast 'live'. (For production techniques for packages, documentaries and features, refer to the relevant chapters.)

In the earliest days of broadcasting all programmes were live. Pre-production was the greater part of the producer's job. Putting a programme on the air was a little like being an orchestral conductor, for whom the live performance is the exciting confirmation of all that has been discovered and practised during rehearsals.

In modern speech-based radio, chat shows with studio guests are likely to be live; magazine programmes, a mixture of pre-recorded and live items; while documentaries are almost always pre-recorded.

In those stations where there is still a choice between modes of production, ardent discussions can be heard about the advantages of live or pre-recorded programmes.

Pre-recorded programmes have the principal advantage of technical perfection. Errors are noted and sections may be re-recorded. No unwanted material should appear.

Live programmes run the risk of error and so produce torrents of adrenalin. Live broadcasting is undoubtedly more 'exhilarating'. That is why some producers of documentary programmes record 'as live', treating the programme as if it was going out on the air and had to come out precisely to time.

The more complicated the programme, the greater the chance of error, and all documentaries, whether live or pre-recorded, need a period for 'rehearsal'. No matter how good your inner ear, you will want a rehearsal to hear for yourself how well the material works and to give yourself time for last-minute adjustments.

For a pre-recorded programme you need a stop-watch, a writing pad, a pen and several copies of the script. One is for the presenter, the second for the studio manager or technician, the third for a programme secretary (if there is such a thing) and the fourth for yourself. For more complicated programmes in the BBC there may be two studio managers, the first to control the mixing panel, the other (the 'second pair of hands') to run tapes and discs. Both require a script.

While the presenter sits quietly in the studio reading through the script, you confer with your SMs, telling them where the tricky sections are in your programme. Once you have explained the overall sound you are looking for, the team check the levels of all the pre-recorded material and discs. You may go into the studio to see whether the presenter is happy.

Once level of the presenter's voice has been taken, you are ready to rehearse. There are two schools of thought about rehearsals. The first believes in stopping the rehearsal whenever a problem occurs. The second suggests making notes of problems and waiting until the end of the run-through before re-rehearsing particular sections. If a rehearsal is going well and there is a sense of 'flow' then it seems a pity to halt it for the sake of a minor change.

Another technique with a documentary is to 'rehearse-record'. This is particularly useful with presenters who do their best work at the beginning of the session. With a little luck the recording of the rehearsal will give you most of what you want and you can include re-recorded sections later. (Of course, other presenters need to rehearse their material several times before it begins to sound free and unread.)

As the producer you are responsible for everything in the programme; the editorial content, the technical level, and the timing. You should have checked the script with the inserts before coming to the studio. Rehearsals are not to acquaint you with the material for the first time.

Technicalities should not be left entirely to the studio staff, The more you know about the techniques of sound recording, the more they will respect your wishes. If a poor quality telephone interview is broadcast, it is your responsibility.

In pre-recorded programmes, problems related to timing can be left to the end of the rehearsal or to the post-production, editing stage. Timing is crucial to 'live' broadcasts.

The major difference between pre-recorded and live programmes for the producer lies in the areas of timing and communication. Because the broadcast must end at a precise second, the presenter relies on the producer to give timings. The producer will have back-timed the programme before going on air and be aware how many seconds ahead or behind schedule the programme is running. This information is communicated to the presenter in a calm, positive manner via the talk-back.

Although the producer may rely on the presenter either to cut or stretch script material on demand, the responsibility for timing is the producer's. The news, five minutes before the end, that the programme is under-running by three minutes is not welcome to the average presenter. Producers are indulged if the programme has a programme assistant who calculates the timings, but the programme assistant cannot be blamed for any error. The buck stops with the producer.

There are techniques involving the use of music to help a programme come out on time; they are dealt with in the Make Mine Music chapter.

Not all production concerns whole programmes. Producers may be called upon to help put together pre-recorded packages, either for their own or someone else's programme. Interviews and talks will also require production.

Even if a producer has the necessary knowledge and techniques to make radio, there is an important quality which cannot be taught. The producer must be able to handle people; people of all stations and qualities, of all levels of assurance or nervousness.

There are producers who rant at their studio team; they usually do less well than the calmer, pleasanter personalities. But, most importantly, the producer represents the radio station as far as contributors are concerned. The producer is the host.

Arranging hospitality for VIPs is less important than general pleasantness of demeanour. Your role is to protect the interests of your 'guests'. You are the professional and your contributors are relying on you for guidance and support.

A useful device is the ghost recording. Sometimes interviewees are very nervous of the studio and all its equipment. In extreme cases you, as producer, may pre-arrange with your interviewer to lead the conversation in the studio gently towards the subject. The cubicle eavesdrops and at the appropriate moment the SM begins to record. Often the interviewee is delighted to discover that the ordeal is over and refuses your kind offer to do it again.

There is something known in the BBC as an ROT. The initials stand for Recording Off Transmission. If you have a live programme which has a repeat edition with no updating requirement then you can record it and broadcast the recording later. If there were 'fluffs' in the live edition, they can be excised from the tape. This is the first kind of...

22.6 POST-PRODUCTION

Another is the editing of second or third editions down to size if the durations of the editions vary. Editing a programme designed for one duration down to another demands a sensitive and ingenious blade.

Post-production tends to be a question of editing, often away from the studio. Many producers are quite happy to chop away at tape machines in their offices. If you do take away a tape for editing, make sure you return it to the point of transmission. The tape will also need some words for the continuity announcer to speak, to introduce and back-announce your programme (unless the programme already contains this information, in which case it is known as 'self-announcing').

Once the final editing has been done, the producer may have to produce programme trail material. Trails are on-air advertisements; they have to titillate the listener's fancy. They may contain an excerpt of the programme or the presenter's voice or both.

They are of paramount importance. Your job is to do everything to ensure that your programme will be heard. (Part of pre-production would have been to prepare advance written publicity for the press and the station magazine.) Too many producers think their job is simply to make beautiful programmes. Publicity is an integral part of the job.

The last part of post-production is boring paper-work. The producer is responsible for ensuring that all the required forms are filled out relating to programme details for copyright purposes. Payments have to be made to contributors and, last but not least, letters composed to thank people for taking part in your programme.

The above description of the producer's duties is not exhaustive. It's impossible to think of every eventuality that a producer might have to face during the course of a day in radio. Local-radio people will be amused by references to SMs, programme assistants and the like. In many modern stations there are not even producers. Presenters produce themselves and control their own technical equipment. On certain stations, formal programmes such as documentaries, features and magazines never appear.

But, apart from differences in names for functions and tasks, the essential qualities needed to be a producer are common to all broadcasting. It is the application of those qualities with sensitivity and intelligence that make any format of speech-radio sound better.

23 RADIO STAR

RADIO is easier to get into than either television or print journalism. That does not mean you can just walk in off the street and get a job (although it's always worth a try).

Radio skills are relatively easy to acquire. With a modicum of talent, intelligence and application you can perfect the basic skills necessary for a speech-based station within three years. Most of those skills are dealt with in these pages and the accompanying tape. But book learning alone will not enable you to broadcast.

It is the linking of formal tuition to opportunity, experience and talent which produces the finished broadcaster.

There are certain qualities which broadcasters need, qualities of mind and temperament. The paramount quality is sound sensibility.

There have been (and still are) broadcasters with what is known as a 'tin ear'; people who regard radio as a script with sounds added.

Their approach to the medium is through the written word. They live in a world of transcribed interviews; they edit not for sound but for vision, excising unwanted tracts on the page, only to discover that the final version doesn't 'sound' right. Such dullards often introduce themselves as journalists rather than broadcasters and treat radio as a training ground for their true ambition, a job in print journalism.

Unfortunately, there were also those in the past who cared only about the sound of their programmes and not enough about good journalism or editorial judgement. They opened the doors to the tough guys who sneer at wimpish 'sound values'.

You won't be surprised to hear that we suggest that a middle course needs to be steered between the two extremes.

The isle of radio is full of noises and the art of radio is the sensitive shaping of noise. Voices, sound effects, music and silence are the materials. Your ears, inner and outer, are the tools for constructing programmes out of them.

23.1 THE JOB MARKET

Although this course is not a career guide for would-be radio people, there's no use in pretending that the question of employment is not at the forefront of many people's minds. So let's look at what there is on offer and whether you fit the bill.

Broadcasters fall into three main groups: generalists, whose specialism is broadcasting; specialists, whose sideline is broadcasting; and composite specialist broadcasters.

It's obvious that there will always be specialists whose knowledge is as important as their radio skills. Newsroom journalists, sports reporters, DJs, correspondents, current-affairs presenters. There is no point in applying for a job as a serious-music producer if you cannot read a score and think the art of composition died with Mahler.

There are also thousands of 'generalist' broadcasters whose specialism is the art of radio. They may be general freelances, selling their skills in as many markets as they can reach. Or they may be local broadcasters, turning their hand (and mouth) to any task an impoverished station throws at them. They may be ambitious producers, eager to tackle ever-more-difficult tasks to reach the highest rung of the professional ladder, where the ultimate skill is in avoiding the fatal fall.

Few people achieve great wealth through radio, although commercial station owners set out with that ambition. A select band of broadcasters achieve national fame through the medium of radio. But real celebrity only occurs after indignant accusations of bias by government ministers, headlined in the tabloid press.

On the whole, radio is similar to publishing in Britain, a profession for the underpaid enthusiast. But because radio can lead to other media jobs it continues to attract young people eager to enlist, in spite of initially low rewards.

23.2 GETTING STARTED

Debutants in radio are caught in the classic 'Catch 22' of the media.

'Could I have a job on your station, please?'

'Certainly. Any experience in radio?'

'No.'

'Sorry. We never hire people without experience.'

'But how do I get the experience, unless someone is ready to give me a chance?'

There are many ways to enter the radio profession. (Even by walking in off the street and asking for a job.) In Britain, the BBC's highest flyers are the production and news trainees. People on these attractive schemes are offered the paid opportunity to move round the various directorates of the Corporation, applying for jobs as they circulate.

There is one snag about becoming a trainee: the competition. A young friend who tried to get into television this way found that all her contemporaries at Oxford University had applied to appear before the same BBC appointments board. Not one was invited.

Advertisements have the signal disadvantage that everybody reads them; as a consequence the field is enormous. Many are not called and very few are chosen. Those who are chosen are not necessarily those with the best academic qualifications. First-class honours graduates do not, on the whole, the best broadcasters make.

The worst part of a broadcasting career is the first step. The big interview will either be with a youth in jeans (and you in your Sunday best) or with a 'board', a group of besuited BBC managers (and you in your jeans).

Potential employers are looking for strong evidence of interest in the medium, the 'right' kind of personality (fresh, relaxed, eager, self-deprecating; an individualist and a good team-worker – the nearest thing to perfection) and an 'X factor', which the board members all claim to recognise.

So much for assaulting the front portals. There are more circuitous routes.

Apart from the occasional genius who has been constructing radio-receivers from the age of three, most of us embark on some kind of formal tuition to learn about the medium a little later in life. Today, courses in radio are being supplied to a growing market, either as part of a media-studies degree or in adult evening-classes. Radio is a growth industry all over the world.

Hospital radio is a useful part-time occupation, socially and personally. You learn to operate gear and gain self-confidence in front of a microphone at the expense of a prostrate audience. The main fare is record programmes, with a request element and interviews with patients and staff. To subsequent employers a stint in hospital radio denotes interest strong enough to survive the presence of the other hospital broadcasters and the absence of any payment.

Local radio or newspapers are other good places to set out. For those prepared to make an affable nuisance of themselves, local radio can usually find a corner. Having offered your services free to the hospital, you are now offered free tickets to those events which would otherwise pass unnoticed and unattended. Eventually one of your pieces makes it to air and you have begun your career in earnest.

Local radio, whether commercial or public service, is a great forcing ground. Because it is generally under-funded it places great stress on versatility and energy. After three years on a station with a true interest in its community, you will have acquired a very wide range of skills. Many of the most confident and successful broadcasters on the national networks started out in local radio.

Not that national fame is necessary for a happy career. Local and regional horizons are often more than enough for the broadcaster who seeks variety within a 'family environment'.

While print journalists are not always impressed with their broadcasting brethren, there is a breathless adulation of print journalists in certain quarters of the broadcasting world.

A couple of years on the more recondite pages of the 'Financial Times' or 'The Guardian' will impress potential employers.

But print journalists with any kind of saleable specialism tend to remain in print and sell their services as interviewees, script writers or presenters to the electronic media. Broadcasting becomes a nice little earner. As it does for other specialists, particularly in the groves of academe.

Naturally, this is far from being the end of the story. In fact, it's just the beginning. There's still a while to go before you can lay claim to the title 'broadcaster'.

This course does not even claim to be exhaustive; we have given you the bare bones of basic theory. It is up to you to flesh them out. Recording and editing equipment may not be at hand but there's nothing to stop you interviewing friends without recording, writing a talk-script or reading that script aloud to work on your presentation. If all else fails, switch on your radio set. Use your ears to measure the programme output against what you have already learned. Find out whether others practise what we have been preaching.

If you and we have done our job together, when the opportunity does arise to broadcast, you will have the confidence of familiarity with the medium, its equipment and techniques. Terminology will not terrify you.

However, a few gaps remain in your knowledge; we haven't got to grips with drama, news, current affairs or outside broadcasts. Enough to fill another volume, in fact.

In the meantime, thanks for reading – and listening to – 'Making Radio'.

And all the best with your broadcasting career.

INDEX

ORDER FORM

FREE CASSETTE WITH THIS EDITION
Around the World in 80 Seconds (48 min. cassette)

Please send my FREE cassette demonstrating the broadcasting of sound effects, the sound environment, handling interviews, talks and microphones, and many other aspects of broadcasting, raised in MAKING RADIO, to:

Name ....

Address ....

....

.... **Postcode**..

Please send a stamped (29p 2nd class, or 38p 1st class)
self-addressed envelope to SANDRA HILL, IMAGES,
THE WELLS HOUSE, HOLYWELL ROAD,
MALVERN WELLS, WORCESTER, WR14 4LH.
Please allow up to 14 days for delivery.